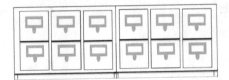

THE TRUE STORY OF BABY

and the Mission She Inspired
to Help Dogs Everywhere

A
RARE BREED
of Love

JANA KOHL, Psy.D.

A FIRESIDE BOOK

Published by Simon & Schuster

New York London Toronto Sydney

Fireside
A Division of Simon & Schuster, Inc.
1230 Avenue of the Americas
New York, NY 10020

First Fireside hardcover edition June 2008

FIRESIDE and colophon are registered trademarks of Simon & Schuster, Inc.

"Crimes Against Dog" by Alice Walker © 2003 by Alice Walker, from *Dog Is My Co-Pilot:*
Great Writers on the World's Oldest Friendship, edited by Bark. Published by Crown.
Reprinted by permission of The Wendy Weil Agency, Inc.

For information about special discounts for bulk purchases,
please contact Simon & Schuster Special Sales at 1-800-456-6798
or business@simonandschuster.com.

Designed by Joy O'Meara

Manufactured in the United States of America

1   3   5   7   9   10   8   6   4   2

ISBN-13: 978-1-4165-6403-4
ISBN-10: 1-4165-6403-9

*There were many who encouraged me
during the challenging process of producing
and writing this book, and I'm grateful to each.
But none more than a dog named Baby,
whose harrowing ordeal inspired it in the first place,
and whose daily presence in my life is all the inspiration
I need to continue advocating for those who have no voice.*

*This is for her, and for all the dogs at puppy mills
who have been forsaken.*

Contents

Acknowledgments

I'm indebted to the generosity and expertise of many people:

Heartfelt thanks to singer-songwriter Bryan Harrell, whose magnificent and inspiring collection of songs is the perfect companion CD to the book (www.bryanharrell.com). For the many photos he also took, not to mention advice and help with the entire project, I'm profoundly grateful.

My deep appreciation to Wayne Pacelle, president and CEO of The Humane Society of the United States (HSUS). As a leader and mentor he's unsurpassed, and I'm blessed to have him in my life. Thanks to all those who work alongside him at HSUS who have earned my respect and admiration, who are my teachers and my inspiration: Stephanie Shain, Kathy Bauch, Michael Markarian, Miyun Park, Paul Shapiro, Mimi Brody, and hundreds of others I cannot name here.

Thank you to my terrific agent, Mary Ann Naples of The Creative Culture, who "got it" from the first moments we spoke.

An awe-filled thank-you to the amazing team at Simon & Schuster, who brought the project to fruition with cheerful and wondrous efficiency: Michelle Howry, Meghan Stevenson, Trish Todd, Mark Gompertz, Chris Lloreda, Marcia Burch, Josh Karpf, Joy O'Meara, Patricia Nicolescu, Emily Remes, Jessica Roth, and Lorenza Galella. I don't know how they manage with such focus and calm the seemingly endless details of so many books.

My everlasting gratitude to the "Drive-by Angel" and "Sarah," Baby's two foster mothers. Without them both, Baby would have perished and this project would have never happened.

A great big thank-you to:

Diane Beifeld, for doing a mitzvah (and even standing in as a photographer)
Relani Belous, for meticulous legal counsel and advice in all areas of the project

Hilary Black, for cookies the celebs *loved* (www.eathilaryscookies.com; 312-285-5055)

Arlene Branca, congressional expert extraordinaire

Dr. Robert Buchanan, for introducing me to the good people at the National Catholic Bioethics Center, and for accompanying me to pick up Baby on my second visit

Lupita Cervantes, Jessica Johnston, Vanessa Chapeton, Liliana Lezcano, Angie Zdandowski, and Margaret Nowak for loving and attentive care of Baby

Leigh Ann Conway, for brilliant oversight of absolutely everything

Jennifer Cranston for the celeb invitations and more (www.cranstoncreative.com)

Danielle Disch, Chicago White Sox, for being so helpful and an enthusiastic dog rescuer herself

Alison Fillmore, for a dazzling proposal (Vervaine Design Studio, www.vervaine.com)

Billie Fitzpatrick, for superb organization of the proposal (www.billiefitzpatrick.com)

Jennifer Graylock, for red carpet photography (www.graylock.com)

Renata Graw, for production help on the celeb invitation (www.renatagraw.com)

Marie Griffin, for celebrity outreach and being a godsend at just the right time (marie.griffin@griffinmarketingpr.com)

Paul Harvey Jr., for brilliant advice and having a heart of gold

Jay Horwitz, New York Mets, for taking great care of me and Baby

Clarice Kogan, for early words of encouragement

Lisa Kohl, for feedback on every area of the project—and beyond

Sidney and Dorothy Kohl, for generous support that enabled me to carry out this project in the manner it deserved

Kris Kelly, tireless dog rescuer (www.thekriskellyfoundation.org)

Nancie King and Ron Mertz, for a gorgeous painting of Baby, and for the photos I will always cherish (www.nanciekingmertz.com)

Richard Levin, Major League Baseball, for putting me in touch with so many animal-loving players

Tara Murphy, an angel who stepped up and said, "What can I do?"

The National Catholic Bioethics Center's Dr. John Haas (president) and Father Tad Pacholczyk, for leadership in speaking out against animal cruelty; and Tara Capizzi for her follow-through

Kathy Petrauskas, consultant and photographer on the celebrity invitation

Wendy Piatek, fearless advocate and cherished friend who shares the vision of a world without puppy mills and the drive to make it happen

Lauren Pronger, for rallying the troops

Moses Robles, Web design (www.oakinteractive.com)

Jody Russell, for being my champion in this and all endeavors

Bud Selig, Commissioner of Baseball, for generous assistance

Stacey Shapiro, for the beautiful calligraphy on the celeb invitations (staceyshapiro@yahoo.com)

Bari Zaki, for stunning presentation boxes for the celeb invitations (www.barizaki.com)

My sincerest thanks to all the celebrities who participated, and to those who work with them who were helpful at every turn: Laura Amazzone, Steven Bennett, Melanie McLaughlin, Melissa O'Keefe, Candy Pantano, Gary Rosen, Teri Thomerson, and Courtney Stewart.

Deepest appreciation to the talented photographers who participated in this project, starting with Robert Sebree, who was there from day one. Please see the complete list of their credits and contact information at the end of this book: Jessica Brooks, Brie Childers, Steve Cohn, Cynthia Daniel, Vange Darling, Larry Ford, Josh Freiwald, Cameron Goodpaster, Steve

Grubman, Bryan Harrell, Gregory Heisler, Gerri Hernandez, Blake Little, Gitte Meldgaard, Jim Newberry, Metin Oner, Kathy Petrauskas, Elizabeth Sagarin, Robert Sebree, Jamie Slade, Tori Soper, Pete Stenberg, David Sutton, and George Tolbert.

Their beautiful and poignant images captured the many wondrous moments of Baby's new life, for which I'll be forever grateful.

Introduction

Wayne Pacelle,
President of the Humane Society of the United States

This book is much more than a story about a girl and her dog. It's a story of two lives changed forever by an act of compassion.

From the moment that Jana Kohl caught a glimpse of a beaten-down, frail, and forgotten nine-year-old poodle, there was no turning away. Jana adopted that old girl who had been rescued from her hardship as a breeding female at a puppy mill in California. And now, with this beautiful book, Jana is going back to help the ones left behind.

The book is about transformation. The author has had a lifelong concern about animal cruelty, but only a more recent awareness of its scope and the acute misery and loneliness so many animals endure at puppy mills, research laboratories, factory farms, and other places where they are treated like commodities or mere objects. With this knowledge, things could never be the same for Jana, and so she has become one of the leading advocates for animals in this nation. She has helped to transform the lives of millions of abused animals, and Baby has been a remarkable motivator.

While serving as a breeding machine at the puppy mill, Baby didn't have a name—just a number. She was number 94, which was tattooed on the inside of her ear. She was one of tens of thousands of breeding females languishing in cages at puppy mills throughout America, and just one of the victims at the puppy mill in California. After nine years, finally a name replaced a number. There are millions of dogs at puppy mills, but they suffer one at a time.

The book is also about remembering. Jana adopted Baby, but she never forgot that she had to leave behind so many other dogs with numbers. She knew she could not personally rescue them all. So she decided she must throw a spotlight on puppy mills, convinced that when enough people learn about these wretched places, reforms in the law will follow.

There is a right way and a wrong way to relate to animals. Baby had been confined and neglected at the puppy mill. In her new life, Baby is out of the cage, a world away from the torments of the puppy mill, in a life filled with kindness and companionship. Now Jana and Baby go everywhere together. I've seen the sight for myself, and it's a beautiful expression of the human-animal bond.

The book is about forgiveness, too. Baby went through so much, and such traumas can affect a dog forever. Her suffering at the puppy mill even led to the loss of a leg. You'd think she'd be bitter or aggressive toward people as a consequence—and you could hardly blame her if she were. But every time I see Baby, I know that I am in the presence of a gentle, loving, and trusting creature. She has all the best qualities of her species, and that says a lot.

In the pages that follow, you'll see images of Baby with many famous and powerful people. She has become a kind of ambassador for all dogs suffering in puppy mills. She reminds us of the life force in every creature and the will to live that is as strong in animals as it is in each one of us.

But for all the power of Baby's story, no one creature can solve the problem of puppy mills and other forms of animal exploitation. It's a human problem—a problem caused by a hard-hearted few—and it is for us to solve with reforms in law. Puppy mills exist because we have allowed greed and callousness to trump kindness and mercy. With better laws and rigorous enforcement, we can close these places down forever.

We are an animal-loving culture, with anticruelty laws in all of the states, more than 165 million dogs and cats in our homes, and annual spending on our companion animals now exceeding $40 billion. There are more sophisticated veterinary medical procedures administered than ever before, and through these often costly human interventions, we are extending the lives of dogs and cats like never before and improving the quality of their lives.

We have Animal Planet on television. Book publishing on animals, animal behavior training, and animal advocacy have never been so robust. And philanthropy for animals is surging, with one successful high-tech entrepreneur now in the process of turning over more than $1 billion toward the plight of homeless pets.

Yet at the same time, animal abuse is rampant. We keep animals in intensive confinement for food production on factory farms. We kill tens of millions of animals for fur, even though we have perfectly viable alternatives. Tens of thousands of people stage dogfights and cockfights and gamble on the outcomes. And, of course, we have the entire puppy mill industry, with perhaps as many as ten thousand of these mills now operating in this country alone. Even as this tawdry industry is churning out more than five million puppies a year for the pet trade, nearly four million healthy and treatable dogs and cats in shelters are euthanized each year because no one would adopt them.

At the mills, the dogs typically live in squalid and overcrowded conditions, housed in wire cages that do not shelter them from harsh winds of winter or the beating sun in summer. The puppies shipped off at eight weeks of age or even younger are often sick as a result of their unhealthy living conditions and their stressful lives. The animals produced by puppy mills are often inbred, and the animals sold through pet stores or on the Internet will suffer for a lifetime with their genetic defects.

With hundreds and sometimes thousands of dogs at a single puppy mill, and just a handful of workers who barely keep up with feeding and watering the animals, there is social deprivation and an utter absence of human attention. As people walk by, the dogs bark and jump, yearning for a gentle pat or a loving word. But there's no such generosity offered, and it would be unthinkable to play ball with them or allow them to sleep in the bed.

Understanding this problem is the first necessary step in solving it. Animal abuse and exploitation may not be the worst of the world's problems, but it's not far down the list in my mind. And when the alternatives to harming animals are so practical and achievable—adopting animals from shelters and rescue groups rather than purchasing them from pet stores and puppy mills—we must not turn away from the responsibility.

This is a magical and poignant and uplifting book, and I hope you will share it with friends and acquaintances. And once you've spent time with it, I hope you will join in helping to solve this problem. Baby showed us how much love and devotion just one dog had to offer. And in puppy mills and shelters across the world, there are millions of others just like her.

A
RARE BREED
of Love

Sometimes I wonder if I'm dreaming.

I open my eyes and find myself in a soft, comfy bed, not a wire cage. The house is filled with sweet, peaceful silence, not the desperate cries of dogs. And then there's her. She calls herself "Ma." After she adopted me I didn't know what to expect. After years of being locked in a cage, I had lost all hope of ever being treated with kindness, but from the moment she touched me, I was smitten. Whenever she picks me up or strokes my head, she is careful, soft, gentle. She doesn't grab me. She never hurts me. She feeds me delicious food, as much as I need to feel satisfied. There is always fresh, cool water in my bowl. She actually kisses me. A lot. And sings to me. And lets me sleep pressed against her. I'm not afraid anymore. I have a name, not a number. I am loved now.

The cast and crew of Spamalot hear Baby's story and offer to help.

Com*pas*sion (n):

The quality of understanding the suffering of others and wanting to do something about it.

Chapter 1

Baby's Story

Just shy of his ninth birthday, my dog Blue lost a year-long battle with cancer, which had begun as a small melanoma on his lip and rapidly over-took his entire body. I couldn't bear to see him suffer. When the day came that he could no longer eat or muster the strength to go for a walk, I called the vet to come to our home. I was filled with angst about whether Blue had suffered too long already, or if he still had some good days left.

As he lay stretched out on the living room rug, very still and seemingly peaceful, I studied his magnificent profile before the doctor administered the injection that ended his life. **Leaning close, I told Blue how much I loved him, and I thanked him for being my most important teacher. I was, and still am, filled with wonder that a member of another species taught me about unconditional love and the inter-connectedness of all living things on this planet.** Although my beloved Blue was certainly my first dog teacher, it was my second dog—a three-legged puppy-mill survivor named Baby—who exposed me to a world I never knew existed, one that would profoundly impact the course of my life.

At first it was hard to think of any dog replacing Blue, but several months after his death, I thought I might be ready to look for another. This time I wanted a small dog, one who could travel with me. I did an online search for toy poodles, which led me to an innocent-sounding website, where hundreds of breeders advertise. I spent hours reading the postings, *oohing* and *ahhing* over all of the adorable pictures of pups for sale, never once suspecting that behind many of those innocent photographs was rampant abuse and unspeakable suffering.

I mentioned my search to a friend who worked in animal welfare, and she was horrified that I would even consider buying a dog from a breeder, especially one from an Internet site. And so began my education into the cruel world of mass dog production. Up until that time, the animal welfare topics that I had primarily been aware of were the inhumane methods of raising and killing animals in the food and fur industries. But I knew nothing about puppy mills. My friend tried to explain that dogs sold at pet stores typically come from inhumane breeding factories known as puppy mills, and that most commercial breeders—no matter what they advertise—are guilty of mistreatment. She tried to sell me on the idea of adopting from a shelter or a rescue group, but I'm ashamed to say that I only half-listened. All I could see were those adorable faces staring at me from my computer screen.

One breeder, in particular, sounded impressive—he was based in Texas, and the picture he had posted of the most darling puppy clinched the deal. I called the number and put a deposit in the mail to him that day. To satisfy my curiosity, and hopefully dispel the worries of my animal-welfare friend, I decided to fly down to Texas to see the breeder's operation firsthand. After landing at the airport, accompanied by my friend Bryan, we rented a car, and about an hour later were parked at the end of a long dirt road that ran beside acres of flat land dotted by a couple of sheds and a house farther in the distance.

It was a Sunday, a fact I'll never forget because we had to wait for the man to return from church. (How ironic, given what we would soon learn about him.) As soon as we stepped out of our car, horrible sounds greeted us—the desperate cries of hundreds of dogs barking from within the two wooden sheds. I felt a terrible sense of dread in the pit of my stomach, knowing this was what my friend had tried to warn me about.

The owner showed us into the smaller of the two sheds, which housed a couple dozen wire cages, a lone and frightened puppy in each one. These were the puppies for sale. The moment we entered, they all flung themselves against the sides of their barren cells, frantic to get out, except for one puppy who lay still and listless in the corner of his enclosure. The fear, loneliness, and deprivation were palpable, and overwhelming. This wasn't the warm and fuzzy, bucolic setting I had envisioned. This was a business, and to the mill owner these puppies were a commodity, no different than soybeans or metal widgets.

The racket from the larger shed next door increased as the occupants obviously sensed our presence. When we asked, we were told that the breeding dogs were kept in there. I couldn't bring myself to go in and asked Bryan to take a look. Minutes later he came out, his face grim. Later he would describe the misery he saw—dogs crowded into cages, trampling each other to try to reach him as he neared, animals who have gone cage crazy, spinning endlessly, others who were gravely ill or severly maimed, some appearing to be near death, all with filthy matted coats covered with urine

Puppy mills: Dogs are imprisoned in cages for life in unimaginably horrific and cruel conditions.

and feces that filled their cages, and the overpowering stench that made him gag—the sights, sounds, and smells of torture and suffering.

Bryan glared at the miller. "You have all this land," he said, "don't you ever let the dogs out of their cages to run around?"

The man shook his head, explaining that he didn't want to be bothered with ants or insects getting on the dogs, or them running away, and that it was easier to keep them in cages all the time.

The idea of an animal being locked in a cage for years was so staggering to me that I felt my chest tighten in panic for them. Thinking money was the issue, I offered to write him a check on the spot to fence-in an area for them to get exercise. He declined. When we told him that we thought it was incredibly cruel, that the dogs were obviously going insane and suffering a horrendous existence, he shrugged and said, "They don't mind being locked up. Animals don't have feelings." He added that he had been inspected by the USDA and was told he had a "model facility."

I replied that if the USDA called this a model facility, the standards had to be changed, and that I couldn't, in good conscience, be a party to it by buying a puppy from him. Bryan, having been raised a Christian, and remembering that the man had been to church that morning, tried to reason with him on those grounds, reminding him that God and the Bible were clear about the need for humane treatment of animals. My own Jewish background taught the same. The man didn't respond to that, unwilling or unable to see anything other than dollar signs where these dogs were concerned.

We drove off, panicked and despondent over having to leave all those tortured animals behind, and aching for the thousands of others who, we now realized, were being abused by breeders across the country. I remember we were both so filled with helpless rage over not being able to take those dogs with us that we couldn't speak to each other for a while. I thought about buying every last dog and taking them all with me, but I knew the man would have restocked the cages with new breeding dogs within a week. I multiplied this mill times thousands that I imagined across the nation and felt a staggering sense of helplessness and despair.

In that instant I knew that this was a defining moment in my life, and that I would never be the same. I remember saying to myself, "Your life will never be the same after today." As I tried to come to terms with the horror that surrounded us, my only thought was: *You must stop this. However long it takes, however much it costs, you must stop this.*

I realized that this was an ugly secret being kept from the public—and obviously supported by the USDA, which, I was to learn, fails to adequately enforce animal welfare standards in many industries. But I would also learn that the meager standards that are on the books are anything but humane: If a dog has food and water, she can legally be locked in a cage for years without the breeder being charged with animal abuse. How can we lock an animal in a cage for life and not call that an act of cruelty? This isn't how man's best friend is supposed to be treated, or any animal for that matter.

Such legalized abuse struck me as a travesty—not only for the animals, but for the humans perpetrating it. By hurting these defenseless creatures, we are hurting ourselves just as much—damaging not just our soul, spirit, psyche, or whatever you choose to call it, but our society as a whole, which becomes contaminated by this kind of legalized cruelty. If it's acceptable for a business to abuse animals, it makes it easier for us as a society to abuse the environment, the poor, women, minorities, children, or any voiceless and vulnerable group. I had come to understand that the abuse of animals wasn't an isolated event that can be shrugged off as a necessary evil, or an unavoidable by-product of big business. It's something that sends shockwaves through everyone and everything, from the factory farmer or the puppy miller to the consumer and even the investor who buys stock in an animal-abusing company. It promotes a culture of abuse and destruction that impacts the quality of our lives on every level.

In short, I realized that what hurts the animals hurts us—not just morally and spiritually, but physically (as I would later learn, the cruel, factory-like conditions at livestock farms contribute more to global warming than all the cars, trucks, and planes worldwide).

As our car headed back to the airport, I broke the silence and vowed that I would do whatever it took to stop this cruelty, starting with rescuing a dog instead of buying one from a breeder. But I knew that would only be the start. I was determined to let every American know about the misery in those windowless sheds in countless backyards across the nation, and in doing so I would try to change the laws. What was now considered acceptable would be exposed for the ugly truth that it is—animal cruelty, deserving of punishment by every court in the land. I knew that taking on the dog-breeding industry would be no easy task, but I didn't care how tough the opposition might be or how great the cost or the sacrifice. I simply couldn't turn my back on those tortured animals.

Over the next year, I would see countless photos and video footage of puppy mills that were all staggering in their brutality and cruelty. My heart and spirit broke every time I saw documentation of the horrors of these breeding factories, where living beings were reduced to machines. Even my faith in God was shaken, not unlike many others who witness abuse day after day. But as many times as I felt despair, I refused to give up. Walking away simply wasn't an option when I thought of those who were unable to walk away.

That horrific and fateful trip to Texas was my crash course in puppy mills, and the desperate cries from those wooden sheds still haunt me to this day. When I returned to Chicago, I contacted my friend who had delivered the warnings about puppy mills weeks before. Now I hung on her every word. She directed me to local shelters, to rescue groups that specialize in certain breeds, and to Petfinder.com and 1-800-Save-a-Pet .com, national databases that match rescue dogs with potential adopters. On Petfinder.com I did a search for toy poodles and almost immediately spotted Baby's picture and bio. There she was, clinging to her foster mother, along with a sentence or two that described her as a puppy-mill survivor. That was all I needed to know.

Baby was rescued from a California puppy mill by a woman whom my friend Brian dubbed the "Drive-by Angel." One day, as she was driving, she saw a PUPPIES FOR SALE sign by the side of the road. For reasons she can't explain, she felt compelled to pull up to the house. The woman who answered the door wouldn't let her in when she inquired if there were any dogs available. She told her to wait outside.

Minutes later she returned with an armload of older, "spent" breeding dogs—as mill owners call those who can no longer produce litters—whom she deposited in an outdoor pen for Drive-by Angel to examine. One of the dogs repeatedly leaped in the air, trying to engage her, begging to be picked up. Her heart broke to see how underweight they all were, their coats filthy and matted. She knelt down to the skinny white dog who was so frantically trying to get her attention, who at that time only had a number, 94, not a name.

"They're too old to produce. I'm going to put them down," said the woman matter-of-factly. "You can have any of them for two hundred dollars." Drive-by Angel pleaded with the miller to reconsider killing perfectly healthy dogs, but the woman was unmoved. In the end, Drive-by Angel was able to take only one dog, number 94, whom her young children named Baby later that day. When I asked why they had chosen that name, she explained: "When I brought her home, everything was a first for her. Grass. Toys. Furniture. My kids said, 'She doesn't know about anything, just like a baby.'"

Drive-by Angel's life was full with work, kids, and other pets, and her thought was to keep Baby temporarily until a permanent home could be found. Just two days after bringing Baby home, as Drive-by Angel was leaving the house, Baby, in her eagerness not to be left behind, jumped off the sofa and shattered her left front leg. For a normal dog this wouldn't have posed a danger, but for a dog who had been deprived of exercise, proper nutrition, and who was overbred, osteoporosis occurs, thinning the bones to the point where even a simple jump off the sofa was too much for that little leg to take. The vet tried to set the leg three different times, but the bones were too thin and brittle to mend and he had no choice but to amputate.

After Baby's leg was removed, Drive-by Angel placed her with a woman I'll call "Sarah" who had fostered countless rescue dogs over the years and was no stranger to nursing homeless, damaged creatures back to health. She knew about the mill where Baby had come from, having seen other dogs come out of there with broken limbs and worse. It is common for small dogs at puppy mills to have their paws caught in the openings at the bottoms of the wire cages, wrenching their legs as they try to free themselves, which can cause fractures and breaks.

When she felt Baby was ready, Sarah posted Baby's picture and bio on Petfinder.com and waited, hoping for the best. Hundreds of miles away, sitting at my desk in Chicago, I was one of only two people who responded. I guess a three-legged puppy-mill survivor isn't high on many people's list for a pet. After reading my application, Sarah called and told me I was welcome to meet Baby in person.

Even though they were halfway across the country, I felt compelled to book a flight to California. Of all the Petfinder.com listings I read, hers was the one I couldn't forget. On some level that I wasn't conscious of at the time, I must have known there was a bigger purpose to my having found her listing, and that this little dog, who had been through so much, was meant to be with me. Once again I found myself in a rental car driving to another small town, located about an hour from the airport. When Sarah opened her front door, two small, white poodles were at her feet to greet me: Spunky and Baby, who was the smaller of the two. She hopped around the room on three legs, looking considerably happier than in her website picture. Clearly she was enjoying life with them. When I sat down, she jumped into my lap and made herself comfortable, as if she knew I was there for her. Other than the glaring absence of her front leg, the first thing I noticed was that she constantly—and I mean constantly—flicked the air with her tongue, a nervous tick she had likely developed after years of being confined in a cage.

Sarah filled me in on as many details as she knew about Baby's past. Inside her delicate pink ear I saw "94" tattooed, most likely the year of her birth. This would have been the breeder's method of checking her "expiration date," when she'd become too old to breed and would be killed.

As Baby looked up at me adoringly, it was hard to imagine the cold-heartedness of the breeder who was ready to snuff out this little angel, still so full of life. I considered the fate of the others that Drive-by Angel had left behind that day. As I gently held up Baby's ear flap to examine the tattoo, I thought of how many people get permanent body art, albeit voluntarily. Unlike an animal, they can brace themselves for the pain, understand the meaning of it, and accept it as something they are willing, even excited, to endure for the sake of the outcome. But for an animal, to be grabbed and tattooed without knowing what she has done to make someone hurt her so badly, why she is being punished, is altogether different.

I don't have any photos of Baby from the time when she was rescued from the mill, but this was taken not long after. Although she was no longer underweight by this time thanks to her two foster moms, you can still see that she's been through hell.

Just as I thought Baby's story could not get any worse, Sarah told me that Baby couldn't bark because the breeders had cut her vocal cords so they wouldn't have to listen to the dogs' constant cries to be let out of their cages. This was later confirmed when I went to the breeder's home myself and she unashamedly boasted about sticking some kind of scissors down the dogs' throats to do the barbaric deed. Like the Texas puppy miller who dismissed the animals' suffering, she remarked, "It doesn't bother them." I held Baby close and looked at Sarah, wanting her to tell me what to do—how to shut down these places. She just shook her head sadly.

The number tattooed inside a dog's ears is often a mill owner's method of checking an animal's "expiration date." At a glance, he can see the year a dog was born and know when she has gotten too old to breed. Instead of getting a birthday cake on her ninth birthday, as many family dogs do, Baby got a death sentence.

As I listened, my anger mounted. I was resolved to do something, but, surprisingly, at the end of our meeting I felt torn about whether to take Baby with me. Much to Sarah's confusion, and my own, I flew back to Chicago without her. Despite the desperate plea in Baby's eyes, I knew I needed more time to summon my courage and prepare for this decision. As I look back, I think I was still grieving Blue's death and wasn't quite ready to allow another dog to come into my heart. Even more, though, I was scared. Would it be hard to take care of a three-legged dog? What about the fact that she was older? I had just lost a nine-year-old dog to cancer, and Baby was about the same age. And would her constant licking drive me nuts? I felt terrible even asking that; after all, it wasn't her fault that she had developed a nervous tick because she'd been abused. But I was still a novice at rescuing dogs and was afraid of the unknown.

Like a lot of people who have never rescued before, I thought of a rescue dog as "used" or having too much "baggage." I worried that no matter how much love, food, or care I gave her, she would never be able to overcome the trauma and pain of her previous life. I realize now that my fears had more to do with myself and my unresolved feelings about my own past than they did with Baby.

I sheepishly gave Sarah some excuse about why I needed more time and wrote her a check to cover expenses for Baby's care. I think she was dumbfounded that I had come all the way from Chicago to California and was going back without her, but she agreed to keep her awhile longer.

A couple of months passed and Sarah was, understandably, getting a bit impatient. She had travel plans and wanted to get Baby settled in the right home as soon as possible. If I didn't come and get her now she'd have to find another home for her or bring her to the shelter where she volunteered. That spurred me into action, and I booked the next flight out of Chicago. I had stalled long enough. This time when Sarah and Spunky greeted me at the door and that little lamb appeared beside them, looking up at me, I knew in an instant that she belonged with me.

"Come here, little mouse," I said, scooping her up (giving her the first of what would be 1,001 nicknames). As I pressed her to my cheek, I couldn't believe I had hesitated. All doubts had vanished. I knew in my heart that she was meant to be with me. I cuddled and kissed her during the entire drive to the airport, promising her a wonderful new life, vowing that no one would ever hurt her again. That night, after a room service feast at her first hotel, she slept pressed against my side. And after two days of round-the-clock loving, the nervous licking completely stopped.

The reactions Baby and I received were dramatic. Whenever I'd take her out for a walk we could scarcely make it down the street without people approaching us. They'd stop in their tracks

After years of standing and lying in a wire cage, a soft bed was like heaven to Baby. Her nightly ritual, when I put her in bed, is to spend several minutes burrowing her head into the fluffy blankets and pillows with delirious abandon before she curls up beside me. More than three years later, I still love watching her do that every night.

or even slow their cars and roll down their windows to ask, "What happened to her?" "Is she okay now?" "Can I hold her?" "Where did you find her?" "I'm so glad she has you. That's one lucky dog."

I'd smile and tell them *I* was the lucky one, that Baby was a precious gift. If I ever got tired of answering the same questions over and over, several times a day, I reminded myself that it was a small price to pay for spreading the word about puppy mills, and a golden opportunity to convince someone to rescue or adopt a dog instead of buying one from a pet store or breeder.

"Are the people in prison for what they did to her?" I was often asked. That was the hardest question for me to answer. I was as perplexed as everyone else as to why we don't have laws that protect animals from the kind of abuse that Baby and countless other dogs endure at puppy mills and backyard breeding facilities. Like the curious strangers who stopped us every day, I wanted to know why it wasn't a crime for people to lock animals in cages for years on end. And how could it be legal for an owner to cut a dog's vocal cords simply because he didn't want to listen to her cries to be let out of her cage? If these practices weren't recognized as crimes yet, I knew from the outrage of the people we were meeting that there was plenty of support to change the laws. Which is what I had made up my mind to do.

Even a talker like me eventually gets tired of repeating the same thing over and over, so I decided to have Baby's story printed on a card to give out to people. By then, I was more convinced than ever that I had to bring this issue to the country's attention, and I thought a good place to start would be to ask animal-loving celebrities and members of Congress to be photographed with Baby for a book. The yesses poured in, and before long, Baby and I were flying to Hollywood, New York, and Washington, D.C., in a whirlwind of photo shoots and meetings with some of our country's most beloved celebrities and influential leaders. Baby, of course, handled it all with her usual dignity, not knowing or caring who was a big shot and who wasn't. In our eyes, if someone promised to help stop animal cruelty, they were a superstar.

Sometimes in our travels and meetings we'd come across someone who didn't seem to care about speaking out against animal cruelty. That was hard for me. I'd get quiet for a long time, trying to understand how anyone could be unmoved by cruelty to animals. I knew that this kind of indifference was at the core of the problem and that only by addressing the reasons for such apathy would we ever hope to end this abuse.

"Not to worry, Baby," I'd finally say, more for my benefit, of course, than for hers. "There are more good people than bad. We will make a difference. I promise you."

I won't pretend that those experiences haven't taken their toll on me. Ask anyone who advocates for abused animals, and they will tell you that on top of having to absorb the horrific images and details of animal abuse—the stuff of nightmares—there's the added trauma of often being discounted or disbelieved by society, or even by certain members of one's own social circle. Those who are in denial about the abusive way society treats animals may range from one's relatives and friends to elected officials and the press. We may be alternately belittled, ridiculed, or altogether dismissed by certain segments of society that are not ready to hear or accept the truth about the ways we legally abuse animals. And that compounds the trauma for the animal advocate. Imagine witnessing a child being abused and then going to the press, to your elected officials, or to someone in your inner circle to tell them, and having them respond with indifference or even rejection. Other social justice advocates don't have to deal with the invalidation, rejection of facts, and outright denial by the public that animal advocates do, and as such, we may understandably suffer from depression, rage, and post-traumatic stress symptoms, not to mention despair over not being able to rescue the victims, whether from a puppy mill, factory farm, or other abusive industry. Taimie Bryant, professor of law at UCLA, has even written a paper, "Trauma, Law and Advocacy," on this phenomenon, and it was of some comfort to me to know that someone had identified and validated the compounded trauma that we often experience:

> *It is, therefore, not only the animals who suffer. An individual who knows the truth of this animal suffering and of society's failure to address it, is harmed by both the suffering and society's disregard. When that person shares her traumatic knowledge with another, his/her reaction can compound the truth-teller's pain. That person has seen something horrible, but when she tugs on someone's sleeve with the words, "This is awful, awful, awful," she is likely to be pitied for her frailty, chided for anthropomorphizing, or avoided for supposedly projecting her own traumas onto animals' experience.*

People of all ages and backgrounds are drawn to Baby, asking to touch her and hold her. They want to love her. I can't tell you how many people have asked me if she's for sale. The first time somebody asked that, I clutched her tighter, appalled by the very idea. Now I'm used to it. She simply inspires that love.

Just the other day, Baby and I had an extraordinary encounter with a man on the street. He was bedraggled and obviously in trouble—from his disheveled appearance and wild-eyed manner, I suspected he was probably

in the throes of a psychotic or drug-induced episode, maybe both. He charged down the sidewalk toward us, screaming obscenities at the top of his lungs and ranting unintelligibly.

I stiffened as he got closer, wanting to pick up Baby and dash to the other side of street, but instead I froze, thinking of the schizophrenic patients I had worked with during my training to become a psychologist. I reminded myself that none of them had ever hurt me, that their enraged outbursts were more about their own terror of the world around them.

Having reached us, the man looked down at Baby on the sidewalk and abruptly halted.

"Oh!" he cried. "What happened to her?" His tone and face were suddenly transformed. He now looked and sounded completely lucid, like a totally different person than the one charging toward us moments before.

"She was abused and lost her leg," I said.

"Oh, no! That hurts my heart," he exclaimed, placing his hand over the spot on his chest.

I was so stunned I couldn't reply.

"You're taking good care of her, right?" he asked, looking at me squarely. "You aren't going to hurt her," he added more as a statement than a question.

I felt my throat tighten and my eyes well with tears for the empathy this troubled man was offering Baby, someone he identified with and wanted to protect, someone who, for that moment, inspired him to put aside his own agony and feel the pain of another. In the two years since I adopted her, I had never seen a clearer example of Baby's transformational power to elicit love, kindness, and empathy even in the face of one's own suffering. It is a power that animals singularly possess to heal the human soul.

"No one will ever hurt her again," I told him.

The average dog is a nicer person
than the average person.

—Andy Rooney

Chapter 2

An Accidental Activist

I was an unlikely dog lover and an even less likely animal welfare advocate. As a girl growing up in Chicago, I'd cross the street if a four-legged creature so much as headed in my direction. To see me cowered in fear, you'd have thought Godzilla was on the loose. It didn't help that my sisters and I weren't raised with animals, other than the all-too-brief period when a marmalade-colored cat we called Tickles had the misfortune to play a short stint as our family pet. Sometime after he was declawed, as punishment for doing on our upholstered furniture what comes naturally to a cat, he ran away.

(No one considered back then how painful and frustrating it is for a cat to have his claws removed, to have the delicate nerves severed and sense of balance compromised, and to be robbed of his tools for defense and mobility, as nature intended. Indeed, I have since learned that the procedure is akin to having your fingers amputated at the first knuckle. Perhaps that was, in part, what drove poor Tickles away. Or perhaps he met his end as a result of being unable to defend himself.) By that time my little sister had developed a severe allergy to him, so his days with us would have been numbered, anyway, which perhaps, in his catlike wisdom, he foresaw.

Our wardrobe was another glimpse into the role animals played—or didn't play—in our lives. I still have an old black-and-white Polaroid that shows my sisters and me lined up in our matching bunny rabbit coats. There we stood, ages five, seven, and nine, furry hoods framing our beaming faces, grinning proudly for our stylish and beautiful mother. Her own collection of furs filled a small closet during the off-seasons, looking exotic and precious in the cedar-lined space.

My sisters and I would eventually inherit some of her coats when she and my dad moved down to Florida. (I got the three-quarter-length yellow mink—yes, yellow—dyed the color of a baby chick, as well as a golden sable, both of which had her initials elegantly embroidered in the lining.) I can still remember the smell and feel of the pelts, so soft and luxurious. The furthest thing from my mind was animal cruelty, or that they had once been the skin of a living, breathing, vibrant creature. My mother may be less than thrilled to know that those coats are long gone from my wardrobe—the yellow mink given to my sister, who also eventually gave up wearing fur, and the sable coat now used as a blanket for a dog.

Shortly after the rabbit-coat photo was taken, our world came tumbling down. My father, the picture of health, collapsed one Saturday morning while playing golf. One of his golfing buddies reported that as he leaned over to address the ball on the seventh tee, he said, "I can't breathe," and fell to the ground. Sudden death, they called it. He was forty-three years old. That April day my mother found herself a widow at the age of thirty-six, with three young daughters. I can't imagine the shock, grief, and despair she must have felt.

From my own eight-year-old perspective, it was a catastrophe beyond measure. Years later, when I was asked by a guy I was dating how old I was when my father died, I made a classic Freudian slip: "I was eight when I died—I mean, when he died."

Two and a half years after my father's death, my mother was blessed to marry a man with two children of his own who remains, after all these years, her adoring and devoted husband, father to all of us, as well as grandfather to my sisters' and stepbrother's children.

The early loss of my father undoubtedly had a profound impact upon me, both in terms of seeing life in a very somber way, as something fragile and fleeting, but also as something to be celebrated with unbridled joy.

Those who know me well see the no-holds-barred silliness right along with the part of me that's deadly serious.

Regardless of the sensitivities that may have developed as a result of early loss and other family dynamics, Lord knows I wasn't born and bred to be an activist of any sort, no matter how worthy the cause. Both in my first and second family, my siblings and I were raised in comfort, privilege, and with traditional values. It was a world in which boys were encouraged to earn law or business degrees, to carry on the success of the previous generation, while girls were expected to find suitable husbands and raise children—certainly not to work in the trenches of some social justice movement. **It was one thing to raise money for charity by attending a black-tie gala; it was quite another to get one's hands dirty by actually working for the cause.**

This attitude may have been surprising, given the fact that we were Jewish and supposed to fulfill the mandate of *tikkun olam*, a Hebrew phrase that means "repairing the world through social action." But in my particular circle, whereas we were taught the importance of giving generously to charity, hands-on activism was not encouraged. Daughters were expected to marry well and live a life of leisure—perhaps serve on charity boards, play golf at the country club, and throw elegant dinner parties for like-minded friends. The problem for me was that I felt like a square peg in a round hole. As much as I wanted to fit in and be like everyone else, I was more interested in reading books than learning how to host chic parties. I do love beautiful things and a life of luxury as much as the next girl—and I can shop-till-I-drop with the best of them—but I needed more and yearned to do something meaningful, though I wasn't sure what or how to go about finding it.

If someone in our circle would have mentioned that something we enjoyed was produced in a cruel and inhumane way, such as veal or foie gras or fur, most of us wouldn't have paid attention, so faithful were we to whatever was fashionable and in keeping with our lifestyle. I'm hardly in a position to throw stones. It wasn't that long ago that I, too, was content to wear, eat, and consume whatever I pleased without a care as to its origins. I remember seeing animal rights protestors in front of fur stores and regarding them as nothing more than a curiosity, wondering why they were making such a fuss.

And yet, as I look back at my early childhood, there were powerful stirrings and flashes of insight into the suffering of animals who were victimized and abused by society. I recall as a child going to a restaurant with my parents and being distraught to see live lobsters in a tank, their claws bound with thick rubber bands. As we stood at the entrance, waiting to be shown to our table, I could see the poor creatures moving in vain, and I was filled with panic for them to be trapped alive like that.

I felt similar dismay when I'd see fish in a bowl or a tank: One day they were swimming free in oceans and lakes, living a life of natural order and purpose. Then, without warning, they were captured and dumped into glass containers, doomed to live out their lives swimming back and forth monotonously, all for our amusement. The sight of city horses dragging carriages behind them also bothered me as a child. My heart ached for them, as I heard the slow and heavy clomp of their hooves against the hard scorching pavement, their peripheral vision cut off by blinders strapped onto their faces, the toxic fumes from the cars filling their noses. How could the driver or his fare not envision the horse in an open field, mane flying, eyes bright and alive? And the sight of a bird in a cage evoked even greater distress: Their wings, nature's wondrous gift for flight, rendered useless. What must it be like for a bird, or any living creature, to spend his life locked in a cage? I wondered. And why, as a child, did I even think about these things?

Years later, I ran into a childhood acquaintance who I hadn't seen since high school. As we reminisced about the old days, she suddenly blurted out, "It always seemed like you felt trapped."

At first I was taken aback to hear such a personal comment from someone I hardly knew—it made me feel scrutinized and exposed. But at the same time I was grateful for her observation, so hungry was I for validation of the feelings I had. Her remark has even greater significance for me today, considering my current effort to help animals who are also trapped.

It didn't take a degree in psychology (which I eventually earned) to help me understand that I recognized myself in those animals; that unconsciously I must have felt like we shared a common fate of being at the mercy of circumstances beyond our control.

Despite these powerful moments when I was struck and saddened by the mistreatment of animals, the rest of the time I chose to live with my head in the sand, preferring not to question the status quo. I simply didn't allow myself to think about it. It wasn't until years later that I would understand the reason for this inconsistency. If I saw the abuse of animals with my own eyes—the lobsters, for instance—it made an impact. Likewise, it was only when my friend Mary Max, wife of artist Peter Max, insisted that I watch a documentary about the fur industry called *The Witness* that I understood why those protesters were so angry. It was only after seeing those horrifying images for myself, of the literal torture of fur-bearing animals that I removed those items from my closet.

I've learned that such is the nature of most people. Unless we see something with our own eyes, we're often reluctant to take someone's word for it. I come up against this phenomenon almost every day as I try to inform people about the abuse animals endure in many industries. I can describe a particular cruelty until I'm blue in the face, but if people don't see it for themselves, they aren't compelled to act or give up something they enjoy, whether fur or foie gras. I share that tendency to trust only what I see for myself.

But what's tougher for me to accept is the person who, even in the face of hard evidence, is still unwilling to make compassionate changes in their life. In that case I can only hope that if enough of the rest of us do the right thing, the others will be swayed. Sad to say, but peer pressure is

Years after working for the Simon Wiesenthal Center for Holocaust Studies, I would find myself at Simon & Schuster's offices to discuss publication of this book. In the gallery of author photos that line the halls I was drawn to the photos of Anne Frank. My work for a Holocaust organization and now animal welfare are connected. I have long been concerned with how cruelty can become sanctioned by society.

often a more powerful motivator than conscience.

When I was twenty years old, I went to work for the Simon Wiesenthal Center for Holocaust Studies, and much later I pursued a doctorate in psychology. I thought that my sensitive nature, coupled with my traumatic loss during childhood, might make me well-suited to helping others heal their own wounds. And while I loved the education and the fascinating knowledge of human behavior, the clinical part of my training made me realize that I didn't have the gift to help patients heal.

Having been in therapy myself, I have observed that certain therapists have an innate gift as healers. It's a rare combination of skill, knowledge, and temperament, and it's very hard to come by in a single therapist. Although I loved setting up an art-therapy class for the schizophrenic adults who were my patients during one of my rotations, I realized that I enjoyed being a facilitator to help them discover their inner artist more than I enjoyed doing talk therapy.

I finished my doctorate and wondered what I should do with the rest of my life. I hadn't found Mr. Right, didn't have kids, and felt a strong yearning to make a difference in the world. But how?

It was about the time that I finished grad school that I received something in the mail from The Humane Society of the United States (HSUS).

I was a contributor, glad to give to a group that was doing good things for animals, but not very motivated to actually read the material they sent. I suppose I worried there would be painful photos inside and, considering that I had a low threshold for that, I just mailed in a check and threw away any printed material whenever it came. I'm not even sure how or why I got on their mailing list in the first place. If someone had told me at that time what my future held, that I was destined to become an animal welfare advocate, I would have told them they were crazy.

I didn't get my first dog until I was in my thirties, and even then I didn't really want one. I had been sharing my Chicago apartment with a beautiful Somali kitten named Mau who, when she grew into adulthood, made me wheeze and itch something fierce, similar to my little sister's symptoms years earlier. After an allergist scratched and poked dozens of holes in my arms, concluding that I was allergic, not only to cats, but also to dogs, trees, and flowers, I felt doomed to a life devoid of nature. Fortunately, I didn't accept his diagnosis. I did concede that Mau had to go, but today I'm glad to report that I live with a cat once again, having discovered I'm not allergic to all of them. The doctor was also wrong about dogs, trees, and flowers, thank God.

After tearfully placing Mau in a loving home, I thought about getting a dog. My instinct told me I wasn't allergic to dogs, but to be on the safe side, I decided to narrow my search to hypoallergenic breeds. I had outgrown my fear of them by that time, but I can't say I was actually a fan either. They were as unknown to me as iguanas or koala bears. I just wanted another pet and I figured a dog was the next logical choice. You'll laugh when I tell you that a dog seemed like a consolation prize after losing my cat. Of course I was about to be schooled, and it was a sweet-tempered standard poodle named Blue who would be my teacher.

If I had to name the single most important lesson that Blue taught me in the years we lived together, it was that nonhuman animals are highly sentient beings who feel a complex range of emotions, just like us, and in many cases much more intensely than us because of their heightened senses and greater vulnerability. Whether happy, sad, bored, scared, embarrassed, jealous, or proud, Blue let me know with facial expressions, body language, and a variety of sounds that communicated his many feelings, moods, and needs. (When the puppy miller told me that animals don't have feelings, I thought of Blue and was appalled by the denial people engage in when they want to make a buck, even if it means hurting others.) A day didn't pass when I wasn't in awe of how incredible it was for two different species to share a home, to communicate with each other, to coexist in harmony, and even to form a deep bond and love. Of course, it shouldn't have astounded me, considering that we are animals, too, but as a city girl who was so removed from animals and nature, the relationship was all the more magical to me.

The other gift that Blue gave me was the ability to extend the love I had for him to all animals. I found myself newly fascinated by the other amazing creatures in the world, and when I learned more about the plight of many of them—how horribly they are often mistreated and exploited by humans—I was devastated and wanted to help. I was so gratified to finally find constructive ways to put my passion to work, as I did when I assisted Chicago Alderman Joe Moore in his courageous sponsorship of legislation to outlaw the sale of foie gras in our city.

I knew that the State of California had passed legislation banning the production and sale of this "delicacy of despair" as it has been rightly called, and that more than a dozen European countries had also banned force-feeding practices, so when Gene Baur of Farm Sanctuary called to tell me that a member of the Chicago City Council was about to introduce similar legislation in my own city, I jumped at the chance to help. With HSUS and Farm Sanctuary as the two lead groups, I was one of those helping on the ground. I met with one council member after another, showing them graphic photos of the torture endured by ducks and geese who are force-fed (a procedure that entails ramming metal pipes down their throats three times a day) to enlarge their livers to ten times their normal size, resulting in broken beaks, torn throats, imploding internal organs, respiratory failure, and even inability to walk.

It was a grueling campaign that met with intense opposition from the Illinois Restaurant Association, and there were eighteen-hour days when I felt numb from the mental and physical exhaustion of it, but every time I thought of the excruciating pain those birds had to endure, I was driven to work even harder for their sake. We were blessed to have the support of Catholic leaders, such as the National Catholic Bioethics Center and Chicago's Francis Cardinal George, who echoed Pope Benedict's strong condemnation of foie gras; Jewish leaders such as

Gene Baur of Farm Sanctuary, Miyun Park of The Humane Society of the United States, and I nervously wait for the vote to be called in the chamber of the Chicago City Council on whether the sale of foie gras in the city should be banned.

Rabbi Asher Lopatin; and many others, including law professor Margit Livingston of De Paul University and Marsha Nussbaum, professor of law and ethics at the University of Chicago. On the historic day of the vote, as I sat in the City Council Chamber nervously awaiting the outcome, accompanied by Gene and Miyun Park of HSUS (I squeezed Miyun's arm so tightly, I'm sure I left her with a bruise), I couldn't help but reflect on how my life had changed since the days of foie-gras-laden cocktail parties.

When the forty-nine council members finally cast their votes in a 48–1 landslide, I was overcome with emotion. To know that I had played a part in passing a law to alleviate the torture and suffering of animals was

The forty-nine members of the Chicago City Council moments before they cast the historic vote to ban the sale of foie gras.

one of the proudest, most fulfilling moments of my life. Never mind that the mayor of Chicago had repeatedly belittled the ban, calling it the "silliest law" he ever heard of, and vowed to repeal it, and that several Chicago restaurants took his comments as a green light to continue serving the dish after the law was passed. In the worlds of politics and commerce, I have learned that greed is often king, and morality an irritating and unwelcome petitioner, quickly dismissed. But thanks to one politician's courage, conscience, and perseverance, the City of Chicago spoke out against cruelty and made history that day. Because of Alderman Joe Moore, Chicago has been heralded around the world, inspiring other cities to follow suit, including Philadelphia, Boston, and New York, where similiar legislation is being discussed.

After the vote, Gene Baur and I took a stroll through Lincoln Park with Baby and ended up at the pond where ducks and geese were swimming, diving, and flying. It was hard to reconcile the images in my head of birds being brutally force-fed with metal pipes shoved down their throats, their livers and stomachs too enlarged to walk—forget about flying—with these much luckier counterparts in Lincoln Park. It was a fitting way to end the day, watching them as nature intended, in all their God-given glory.

The foie gras campaign had temporarily taken me away from this book, but after the vote I was back on track and eager to put the same effort and energy into stopping puppy mills—I'd seen the impact that a few impassioned advocates could have to change the law and make a difference. I knew, though, that stopping puppy mills would take a big gesture—one that would have to raise national attention. I decided the only thing to do would be to embark on the schlep of all schleps—a cross-country walk from California, where Baby was kept prisoner, to the steps of the U.S. Capitol. My sole companion on this journey would, of course, be the voiceless three-legged dog named Baby who has managed to turn my life upside down—or right-side up, depending on how you look at it.

As I envisioned myself pushing her dog stroller (a necessity due to her handicap) across America, perhaps joined along the way by other puppy-mill survivors and their human rescuers, I also imagined the surprise of those who knew me as someone who was supposed to be living a very different life. But to my way of thinking, there is only one purpose to having wealth or fame, and that's to ease the suffering of others. The moment I saw the hell of a puppy mill, the torture and misery of innocent creatures locked away for their whole lives, I was forever changed—and it left me with a single thought that I heard like a mantra: *What choice do I have?*

Baby, this formerly "disposable" creature, lives a life of comfort now, just as she should. After suffering years of abuse, I wanted her to know that humans can be the source of pleasure, not pain. I am mindful of Baby's needs—for example, building an awning at our previous home in

A stroller comes in handy when Baby gets tired. After walking a while, she'll sit down and look at me, as if to say, okay, enough with the walking.

Chicago so that when the weather was harsh, she wouldn't have to go in the pouring rain or icy snow to relieve herself. Or driving long distances instead of flying so that she won't be re-traumatized by being locked in a small carrier.

That's what happened on Baby's first flight from California to Chicago, when she had diarrhea the entire trip because she was so terrified to be put in a small space again. Due to an unsympathetic flight attendant, our trip home was a disaster. She wouldn't let me take Baby out of the carrier to hold her on my lap, despite my warnings that Baby might get sick from the stress of being enclosed in a small space. Sure enough, after several minutes of frantically thrashing about, trying to free herself from the confines of the carrier, Baby began to have explosive diarrhea.

As I rushed the carrier into the bathroom to clean it and her up, I pleaded with the flight attendant to let me take her out for the rest of the trip. My seatmate came to our aid and tried to convince her, too, but to no avail. As a result, I spent much of the time in the tiny bathroom, sitting on the closed lid of the toilet, with Baby on my lap, or alternately on the postage-stamp-size floor, where she continued to empty her upset stomach. It was summer and I had worn open-toed sandals. I'll never forget looking down to see a splatter of diarrhea across my toes. Needless to say, it was the last time I would fly commercially with her. I refused to put either one of us through that again.

I know I'm not alone in my doting ways. **Surveys show that an overwhelming majority of people use baby talk to communicate with their pets**—that high-pitched singsong tone of voice, accompanied by silly, made-up sounds and words used by mothers (and fathers) the world over when speaking to their human infants and young children. President Bush has admitted to it when talking to his dog, Barney. I also know that countless people refer to themselves as "Mommy" and "Daddy" when talking to their pets. If you're one of those, don't be embarrassed—you're in good company. Judge Judy does it with her dogs, too (her "babies," as she calls them).

One survey found that 80 percent of us consider our pets to be cherished members of the family. The Katrina disaster proved what a fierce attachment we have to our companion animals, when scores of people refused to leave their pets behind during evacuation and rescue efforts, even at risk to their own lives.

A few weeks ago I witnessed a delightful example of this powerful love that we have for animals. A thirtyish mother was pushing a child's stroller down the street, her toddler in tow. As they passed, I did a double-take when I saw that inside the stroller there was a fifty-pound tan dog. The toddler walking beside it was crying. It was a sunny winter day and the little girl was bundled up in a puffy, pink snow jacket, looking like an overstuffed doll with her arms sticking out from her sides, the way all kids look in winter wear. She pointed at the dog in the stroller, sobbing her indignation that her seat was occupied. The mother stopped walking and leaned down to her daughter to explain, "Remy isn't feeling well and he's having trouble walking. We have to take care of him now just like I take care of you when you're hurt. I know he appreciates you letting him use your stroller until we get home." The toddler's whining abated slightly, as the mother then calmly continued homeward, one hand pushing Remy in the stroller, the other holding onto her daughter's pink-mittened hand. (The mother and I crossed paths some time later and she told me that Remy had died of cancer shortly afterward.)

Undoubtedly you've demonstrated similar acts of love or even sacrifice for your animals. When they are sick or hurt you fuss and worry over them, when they're frightened or threatened your instinct is to protect them. You give them their favorite foods, toys, and a warm place to sleep, which is, according to surveys, most likely in bed with you. Many of you even hang a stocking for them on the mantel at Christmastime. In return, they give you unconditional love like nobody else ever has or will, they help you fight diseases like depression, anxiety, high blood pressure, and can even detect cancerous tumors in time to save your life; they wake you up in the middle of the night to tell you the house is on fire; they are the eyes, ears, hands, and feet for those of you who are disabled; and they are the protectors of your house and even of your human children. Is it any surprise, then, that we look into their adoring faces and marvel at the uncommon quality of this relationship, one that we could easily categorize as love? Or that we would readily protect them in the face of the horrific abuse that many of them are enduring even at this moment?

As I have traveled the country, Baby has become a living symbol and an inspiration to hundreds of people who have heard her story, many of whom are political leaders and celebrities who have shared their own stories of a loved dog, posed with her in a photograph, or both.

A Rare Breed of Love is a testament to Baby's seemingly transcendent ability to inspire love and compassion, and also to motivate people to act on behalf of all those dogs who are still imprisoned numbers, as she once was.

Baby and I have also had the honor to meet many unsung heroes who have inspired us with their own acts of mercy on behalf of animals. You'll meet them, too, and be uplifted by the compassionate way they are changing the world for the better.

Baby's power to elicit poignant photos, beautiful smiles, and endearing personal stories from others is a testament to the enormity of our love for dogs, and for animals in general. It is a love that we should be proud to demonstrate, as St. Francis and Abraham Lincoln did, and as the men and women in this book do.

This book celebrates the magical and wondrous relationship so many of us have with members of another species. Those special beings who suffer our foibles and witness our failures with them and with our own kind, who, though they have four legs (or three) instead of two, though they bark instead of use words and catch balls in their mouths instead of their hands, though they are one kind of animal whereas we are another, nevertheless inspire in us . . . a rare breed of love.

Until man extends his circle
of compassion to all living things,
man himself will not find peace.

—Dr. Albert Schweitzer

Chapter 3

Home Sweet Home

Baby reveled in her new life with me in Chicago, arctic Midwest winters and all. Though she was nearly ten years old when I got her, she looked and acted like a puppy—running and skipping ahead of me with glee, but unlike a puppy, stopping every few feet to make sure I was with her every step of the way. If someone had told me about the thrill of adoption, I would have done it years ago. It was such a high that I actually felt selfish—like I was the one being rewarded (which is, in fact, the case). As I watched her prance with joy, I wished everyone could know the sheer delight of rescuing a dog. There is nothing so gratifying as witnessing a dog's happiness over having found their forever home.

I adored my dog Blue, who was an extraordinarily smart, gentle, and magnificent creature, but Baby touched something in me that was so profound and powerful that I found myself overwhelmed with even more intense feelings. The bond I quickly forged with Baby is one that is reserved for the special relationship between rescuer and rescued. It's a bond I hope each of you will experience if you never have, because it has the power to change your life and your soul in ways you can never imagine. Forget about it being a noble act, although it is. There's a selfish payoff to rescuing and caring for an animal in need. It just feels wonderful. I think acts of mercy feel good to the giver because they are God's sneaky way of positively reinforcing us to do good things for others. Giving becomes a feel-good kind of addiction. Plus, and this isn't a widely known fact yet, shelter dogs have the most delicious-smelling toes, exactly like fresh-popped popcorn. I kid you not.

So this is what the world looks like. You can imagine, after Baby had stood on a wire-bottom cage all her life, how glorious the grass must have felt beneath her paws and how wonderful the sun must have felt on her face. To see her running, her face lit up with joy, makes me want to cheer, but at the same time I grieve for all the countless number of dogs still locked away, who will never know the simple God-given right of every living being to run and walk outside.

How incredible it must have felt for Baby to be bathed after years of lying in a filthy cage, covered in excrement and urine. Dogs at puppy mills, doomed to a life of confinement, can never escape the filth from their own natural bodily excretions and that of other dogs. The stench of a barn filled with caged animals is unbearable, both for the human observer and the animals themselves. Undercover investigators have reported that upon entering these sheds or buildings, their eyes stung so badly that they couldn't keep them open, and they gagged from the overpowering stench.

Those first days, as she still does now, she snuggled up to me on every occasion, nestling into my neck or pressing against my side, crawling on top of my chest so that we were nose to nose and then staring into my eyes so deeply and with such emotion. Her lower jaw shifts slightly so that her mouth sets into a questioning curve, as if to say, *Where have you been?* It broke my heart when I first saw the extent of the deprivation and need in her eyes, and the gratitude she showed for the bounty that she now had.

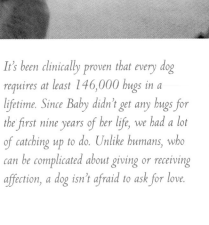

It's been clinically proven that every dog requires at least 146,000 hugs in a lifetime. Since Baby didn't get any hugs for the first nine years of her life, we had a lot of catching up to do. Unlike humans, who can be complicated about giving or receiving affection, a dog isn't afraid to ask for love.

I'm not embarrassed to say that before long I was head over heels in love with this little angel, so full of life and love after all she had been through, so completely forgiving and ready to love a human after what they had done to her. To this day, I'd rather stay home and cuddle with her than go to the hippest party or the most happening event. The simple joy and fulfillment I get from snuggling with a warm and loving creature like Baby is one that I know you understand and share. Gotta go get me some right now . . .

I knew that that first winter in Chicago would be a shock to Baby's system (it still is to me, even after all these years!), so I got her this little parka with faux-fur collar. Every time I put it on her I could hardly stand

Everywhere we go we get stopped by people of all ages and backgrounds. These kids were in Chicago's Lincoln Park and had a hundred questions about Baby.

The U.S. National Parent-Teacher Association Congress has said: "Children trained to extend justice, kindness and mercy to animals become more just, kind and considerate in their relations with one another. Character training along those lines in youth will result in men and women of broader sympathies; more law-abiding in every respect, more valuable citizens."

it—it was the cutest thing I ever saw. For less blustery days I got her this cozy red vest.

No, she doesn't have a diamond collar or a wardrobe of clothes. I'm not a fan of dressing up animals, unless they need an extra layer to keep warm in winter. I once saw a woman with a small dog who was wearing tennis shoes. It never ceases to amaze me that people who profess to love their pets subject them to all sorts of discomfort. The poor animal looked miserable (not to mention absurd), his sensitive pads and paws constricted in leather. I believe that animals deserve to be respected on their own terms and given what they need to thrive, not to be used for our own needs that we selfishly project onto them. I have no doubt that the woman with the shoe-wearing dog was a kind person. She just didn't stop to think about whether shoes might be unnatural and uncomfortable for dogs. They looked cute or trendy and that was good enough for her.

I don't see Baby as a surrogate child who I have to dress up in cute little outfits. She is a dog whose needs I respect, meaning I try to find creative and resourceful ways to help her when I can. I have a stroller for her because as an amputee and a senior she gets tired more quickly than a younger, four-legged dog. Although I'm well aware that she's not a human baby, make no mistake, she is *my* Baby.

I adopted Kitty Pie (formerly known as White Socks) a few months before Baby. Although I thought I could never live with a cat due to my previous allergies, I was thrilled to discover that I didn't have a reaction to Kitty Pie. I adore cats and am grateful to my neighbor Teri Bess, who brought him into my life. At age fourteen, he was senior, too. Kitty Pie wasn't overjoyed when Baby arrived, but he's such a sweet boy that he never took out his disappointment on her.

The two don't interact much, but neither are they enemies. I had hoped one day I'd come home to find them asleep in each other's arms, but the best they've managed is that Kitty Pie let's Baby lick his food bowl clean when he's through. She stands there waiting as he has his fill, then swoops down and gobbles up anything he's left behind. There were many days when she went hungry at the puppy mill, so she isn't about to let even a morsel go to waste.

Baby isn't thrilled when I dote on Kitty Pie. If I cradle him, brush his coat, or clean his tush (he's too chubby to do it himself), she looks forlorn. (Sibling rivalry isn't just a human phenomenon.)

Many animals have an extraordinarily powerful sense of smell. Studies have conclusively shown that dogs can detect cancerous tumors with greater accuracy than machines, predict seizures in eplileptics, and warn of insulin shock in diabetics. Rats can indicate the exact location of land mines, and cats are able to smell impending death, as was the case at a nursing home where the resident cat would consistently perch on the beds of patients who were about to die, thereby predicting their deaths with bizarre precision.

As such, it isn't surprising that dogs can detect changes in hormone levels or stress chemicals that we may produce when we are upset or when we work

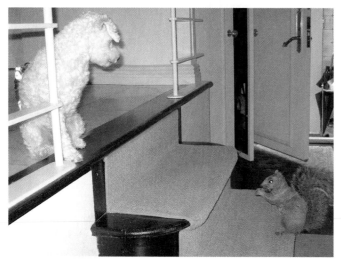

too hard, the latter which was often the case for me over the past few years during this project. Many times Baby would come up to me and nudge me to stop. At first I thought that perhaps she was hungry or needed to go outside to relieve herself, but after ruling those out, I realized that she simply wanted me to stop. I'm convinced it was because she could smell my stress levels, which were undoubtedly off the charts!

Just as the children of the Drive-by Angel observed, everything was a first for Baby, including meeting other animals. Irving the squirrel used to come to our front stoop for breakfast every morning, until the condo board passed a rule prohibiting us from leaving nuts and seeds outside for the birds and squirrels who liked to visit our tree-lined street. For those of us on the lane who were big animal lovers, this was sad. For a time Irving came inside the house to eat so that there wouldn't be any crumbs left outside.

One of the women who was in favor of banishing the squirrels from the lane told me that she didn't like animals and was glad that an exterminator had been called to poison the rats that had been seen scurrying about. I wasn't keen on having rats in the lane either, but as I thought about the horrible and painful end they were about to meet, I wondered aloud why humane traps couldn't be used instead. I gently reminded her, in reference to her "I don't like animals" comment, that we are animals, too.* At that, she looked at me as if I had three heads.

I imagine she was thinking that we are not like "them," that we are smarter and superior. I would have liked to tell her that nonhuman animals are often far superior to us—they can outrun us, outjump us, outsmell us, fly through the air without the aid of a jet engine, and predict earthquakes. And I don't know a single human who can sniff out cancerous tumors. I would have also liked to mention that squirrels such as Irving are ranked among the smartest animals, along with crows, pigs, and yes, even rats. Sometimes, though, I get tired of explaining things to people who are impossibly arrogant about the superiority of the human race. Yes, we can write novels and perform open heart surgery, but nonhuman animals can do a whole lot of things better, faster, and more accurately than we can.

Another first for Baby was birthday cake (vanilla only, of course). At a party for the son of a dear friend, Baby marched over to the kids' table to see if she could get in on the action. She's a chip off the old block in that department.

* I've come a long way. I used to scream when I'd see a spider, then smash it mercilessly. Now I do the glass-and-paper removal method (put a clear glass over the critter, then slide a piece of paper under the glass and carry him outside—a life spared! Plus, you don't have to clean smashed guts off the wall). In my pre-enlightened life I also killed a rat. I had found tiny black droppings in the basement of my house and had asked my housekeeper to buy traps. As I lay in bed that night, I heard an awful *snap!* from two floors below. To my total surprise, instead of feeling relieved, I felt devastated and knew I had done a terrible thing. The sound of the metal bar whacking that rat, and the image of him trapped and bleeding in that contraption, made me sick and filled me with pity and remorse. Today I would use only a humane trap, so that the animal could be relocated to the woods. I'll kill a mosquito if one's about to bite me, and wouldn't hesitate to do the same to any animal who posed a threat to me or anyone else, but my definition of what constitutes a threat has changed to reflect the truth, not just my fears. Rats, by the way, are highly intelligent and sweet, as I would later discover when I visited a ranch in Wyoming, where the ranch hand and his family had one as a pet. The little animal crawled up my shoulder and rested there, as sweet and affectionate as a tiny dog. It made the memory of what I had done all the more painful.

PAUL HARVEY, Radio Personality

I was at a charity event for HSUS and one of the auction items was the chance to meet radio legend Paul Harvey at his recording studio. It was a silent auction, the kind where you write your name and the amount of your bid on a piece of paper. Several people lined up to write bids, but I stood patiently to the side and simply upped the bid after each one. Finally, it was a bidding war between me and a man, and at one point I just turned to him, laughed, and said, "Look, I'm not going away. I'm writing a book to raise awareness about puppy mills and I really want to meet Mr. Harvey to ask him to be in the book, and I'll stay here until dawn if I have to." Fortunately he laughed back and graciously stepped aside.

Indeed, meeting Paul Harvey was a once-in-a-lifetime privilege. That rich, distinctive voice that millions of Americans have trusted for generations is what you expect to notice first, but it's the kindness in his eyes that is most arresting. As a bonus, I got to meet his multitalented son, Paul Harvey Jr., the award-winning producer and writer of the show as well as a broadcaster himself. Both father and son share a deep sensitivity for the suffering of animals and speak out against animal cruelty at every turn.

Paul Harvey is not only one of our nation's treasures—a man who has received awards and keys from cities too numerous to count, as well as the Medal of Freedom from the president of the United States, he is also a man with a heart of gold, a true humanitarian who has been a voice of reason, decency, and conscience for generations. He will celebrate his ninetieth birthday this year, and I add my heartfelt wishes to those who will be sending him greetings and tributes from across the globe (his broadcasts are heard on over twelve hundred stations and read in more than three hundred newspapers.)

As the longest-running and most popular series in radio history, "The Rest of the Story" is also one of timeless content. The piece he gave me to include in this book is classic Paul Harvey—warm, wise, and wonderful. I feel so lucky to share it with you.

"*Priorities*"
by Paul Harvey

This is partly personal . . .

*If your heart is burdened most by the starving babies of
Sub-Saharan Africa, I will respect that.*

*If you lose sleep worrying about brutality within our prisons,
I will respect that and do what I can to help.*

*If you are most anguished by the world's ceaseless wars or by
the prospect of a nuclear one, your preoccupying priority defends itself.*

Will you then allow me mine?

*My nightmares relate all of man's inhumanity to man—
to our willing acceptance of cruelty to the other animals.*

*Somebody once sent to my attention a "humane mouse trap."
The label promised that the "mouse dies in his sleep
without pain or suffering."*

Before recommending it, I researched it.

*I learned that the mouse smells peanut butter inside,
enters the plastic box, and is trapped inside.*

*A spokesperson for the product said that 2½ years of testing
had proved the mouse panics and dies of fright.*

*Or—because the area is so tiny, the mouse from hyperactivity
works up a sweat and dies of heat prostration.*

This, the label describes as "without pain or suffering."

So much for truth in advertising.

I am going to try to be as dispassionate as possible about this.

*I do not mean to suggest that it is but one step from
suffocating animals to putting people in ovens.*

It's not.

It is several steps.

The first step begins with tolerating any pain which we cannot
ourselves feel.

Anguish is anguish. It knows no gender, no race, no species.

Pain is pain.

*If it is your own child who is suffering,
you relate especially to his or her hurt.
Any hurts to others—yourself included—
are comparatively insignificant.*

It is not that your child is suffering any more . . .

Perhaps your child is suffering less . . .

than a mouse suffocating in his cramped dark coffin.

Your child is tortured, that is "hideous—a high crime!"

A mouse dies in agony—that is "pest control."

And there are options.

*So somebody allowed it to happen. Confronted with the options of allowing
the mouse to die in peace or pain, somebody had to say, "What's the
difference?"*

There are equally effective options.

*And civilization should have reached the point at which we should care which
is which.*

*When it comes to suffering, the only thing which separates the smartest of us
from the dumbest of them is our vocal cords.*

*If we allow them to hurt only because they cannot speak,
may God have mercy on them—and us.*

Robin redbreast in a cage
puts all of Heaven in a rage.

—WILLIAM BLAKE

The sight of any animal locked in a cage is very painful to me. And birds, whom nature gave wings to fly, are for me among the saddest of captives. One day Baby and I went into a bead store and saw a tiny cage in the back corner with two small, yellow birds in it. I wanted to cry at the sight of them in that little prison. Not wanting to put the store owner on the defensive, I gently asked her about them.

Her daughter, who ran the shop with her, told me that they had received them as a gift a couple of years ago. I asked if they ever thought about their captivity and the fact that they had wings to fly. The daughter said that she and her mother simply loved the birds and had never thought about that. But as we continued to talk the mother finally chimed in, saying she agreed that it was sad for them to be locked in a cage. I asked if they might consider letting me take the birds to an aviary or a sanctuary where they could fly. They wouldn't be completely free, as they had been in whatever tropical country they had been captured in, but it would be better than their current existence in a sixteen-inch cage.

To my surprise, the mother and daughter both agreed. I went home and immediately researched the options, eventually finding a local man who had set up the interior of a second home as an aviary for neglected and abused birds. Some of the birds had come from people like these women, who had realized that keeping birds in cages was cruel. Before the man agreed to take the birds, he wanted them to be checked by a vet so that the other birds wouldn't be at risk to catch anything. It ended up being an all-day affair and a few hundred dollars for the vet. For the briefest moment, as I sat with the birds in the waiting room of an animal hospital way out in the suburbs (it was the only one I could find that had a vet

qualified to care for exotic animals), I asked myself why I had signed up for this. After all, think of the millions of birds in cages around the world—helping these two hardly made a dent.

But when I finally took them to the birdman's makeshift aviary and he released them into a large room, set up with perches and enough space for them to fly for the first time in years, I knew why I had gone to all the trouble and expense. I recalled that when I was a little girl, a bird accidentally flew into our garage. Someone had the brilliant idea to put him in a cage and keep him in our house as a pet. Ironically we named him Lucky. Hardly. One day shortly after we captured him, we found him lying dead at the bottom of the cage. Thankfully and mercifully, no one felt inclined to replace him with another.

Baby and I on Capitol Hill, meeting with members of Congress.

Cowardice asks the question, "Is it safe?" Expediency asks the question, "Is it politic?" Vanity asks the question, "Is it popular?" But conscience asks the question, "Is it right?" And there comes a time when one must take a position that is neither safe, nor politic, nor popular, but one must take it because one's conscience tells one that it is right.

— MARTIN LUTHER KING JR.

Chapter 4

The Journey Begins

I felt our journey should begin in Washington. I knew it was important for the men and women elected to Congress to meet Baby and see firsthand a living example of the cruelty of one of our nation's industries, monitored and licensed by a governmental agency, the U.S. Department of Agriculture (USDA). As I would eventually learn, the USDA is doing a poor job when it comes to enforcing animal-welfare laws. There are two main problems. First, the laws that are on the books are pathetically minimal in their standards. If a dog has food and water, a miller can legally lock her in a cage her entire life and breed her every heat cycle until she is old and worn out, at which time he can kill her or even auction her off to a broker who will sell her to a research lab. Hard to believe this is legal, right? And second, the USDA more often than not doesn't enforce even the paltry standards that do exist, because, some say, it doesn't have enough funding to provide enough inspections of these businesses. Others say that even when inspections are done, they are meaningless because the standards of care are virtually nonexistent.

I hoped to impress upon members of Congress that the laws we had in regard to puppy mills were grossly, and even criminally, inadequate and should be changed. Yes, criminally, because if you or I were to treat the family dog the way these puppy-mill owners treat breeding dogs, we'd be accused of animal cruelty.

I didn't have any particular skills as a lobbyist. I just decided to present the facts plainly, with Baby as physical evidence. I believed that was all that was needed to make an impact.

And that's what happened. Every senator and congressman we met with, regardless of political party, was outraged and saddened by Baby's story. Quite a few were unaware of the conditions at many dog-breeding facilities and were in agreement that these places should be shut down. Yes, *shut down.* The language they used was not vague or politic or wishy-washy, and it gave me hope that we might have a real chance to either abolish commercial dog-breeding practices as they currently exist at puppy mills or at the very least enact major—and I mean *major*—reform. We cannot settle for anything less, if we're to call ourselves a civilized and humane nation.

In fact, the inhumane confinement practices used in other industries, which are similar to those used at puppy mills, are already under fire. The public has become aware of the cruel confinement practices in the egg industry, and people are increasingly demanding that battery cages for hens be abolished. Several egg-laying hens are crammed together so tightly in a cage about as big as a sheet of paper, unable to open their wings or turn around. Farmers debeak the hens so they won't peck one another to death.

And the hog industry's use of gestation crates for pregnant pigs has also come under fire. Voters in Florida and Arizona were outraged when they learned about the cruel confinement stalls, so narrow that sows cannot turn around, and voted to ban them. Similar reforms are under way in the veal industry, with the owner of the nation's largest veal producer in Wisconsin admitting that taking a baby calf from its mother and tethering him by the neck to a crate in which he cannot take steps or turn around is cruel and inhumane. This veal producer is now voluntarily phasing out veal crates.

But there has been no progress in the dog-breeding industry, even though the lifetime confinement of breeding dogs in cages is no different than these other cruel practices. I felt that the precedents being set in all these other industries would pave the way for reform in this one, too. No animal should be confined to a cage twenty-four hours a day for years on end—it is sheer torture, an act of such extreme cruelty that it should be a criminal offense. Animals go insane when confined, just as we would. They alternate between frantic desperation—flailing about, flinging themselves against the sides of their cages, and engaging in repetitive acts of frustration—or they lie in a corner in a state of hopelessness and utter despair. How can we condone this?

Puppy Mills: A National Disgrace

At so many of the nightmarish facilities known as puppy mills, commercial kennels, or the benign-sounding "backyard breeder" hundreds of thousands of puppies are born and sold each year in conditions that are nothing short of barbaric.

Innocent-looking barns and sheds that dot the landscape of a puppy mill owner's property belie a nightmare inside: Like all animals who are constantly confined, dogs are psychologically scarred from years of imprisonment, going "cage crazy," throwing themselves against the bars, self-mutilating, or becoming lifeless and catatonic. Cages are stacked on top of one another, the urine and feces dripping onto the dogs below. The overpowering stench in these facilities burns the eyes and causes gut-wrenching nausea, as reported by rescuers. Some rescued animals are

A lonely dog locked in a wire cage at an Amish puppy mill in Pennsylvania, while another dog is kept chained to an outdoor post. Sadly, the Amish operate large numbers of puppy mills in Pennsylvania, Ohio, and Indiana.

Grassy areas lie tauntingly within view. Dogs freeze in the winter, losing limbs to frostbite, or die of heatstroke in the summer. Newborn puppies have been reported to literally "cook" on the wires of the cages in the summer.

found wearing collars that have become too tight and are embedded into their necks, which then must be surgically removed; other animals have broken limbs, heartworm, tumors, and a host of crippling diseases and illnesses. Dogs who are kept in complete darkness go blind.

Female dogs are bred the first time they come into heat and every cycle thereafter. When their poor, worn-out bodies can no longer reproduce, they may be shot, left somewhere to starve, clubbed over the head, or sold to medical research laboratories. Most of the puppies you see in pet stores and on Internet puppy sites typically come from these inhumane breeders and mill owners.

When Commerce Is Cruel

The following report was written by an undercover puppy-mill investigator.

Nothing could have prepared me for what I witnessed that day. It began in the first building I entered. There were dogs everywhere crammed into wooden boxes that were no more than 5'x3' in size. There were five or more dogs in each box, stepping on each other to get to the end for me to touch. There was one box full of Chihuahuas and one very tiny, very pregnant girl who was being trampled to death. There were dogs that were very ill and needed vet care. Row after row of these makeshift boxes stood in a small building with no windows or ventilation.

I left that building and walked around to the back side of the building and found larger dogs outside in pens that were in mud holes with empty food and water dishes. Some did not even have dishes in their pens. As I walked by them they all just begged at their fences for me to come and give them a soft touch of a human hand, and maybe they were hoping I had some food for them to eat. In another building I remember one Boston Terrier that will stay with me forever. His eye was so swollen with infection it hung out of his head, the size of a plum. Many of the Bostons had severe cherry eye. Others were so matted and grown out I could not tell what breed they were. There were dogs with cuts and wounds that were infected.

"Emmy," left, as she appeared when rescued from a puppy mill, and right, after a year of love and care in her forever home.

There was no end to the horrors I saw that day. And the stench that took my breath away and made my eyes burn. I just wanted so badly to free them all. Even out in the wild they would have a better chance of survival. How these millers sleep at night I will never understand, for each night I go to bed I still see the same picture in my head of all these poor innocents begging for me to take them out. That day will be embedded into my heart forever. I whispered to them that I would be back.

Here is another investigator's testimony . . .

I will forever be haunted by a Terrier mom with one tiny pup in a small box. The mother was frantically jumping for attention, but she was stepping on the pup. The miller kept screaming at her to stop and said that the other pups were trampled to death by the mother dog. I walked a little farther down the rows of dogs, hoping that if I moved away the dog might stop jumping and the miller would stop screaming at her. The screaming continued, and as I turned I saw the miller pick up a long wooden board and raise it over his head. The miller noticed me watching, and as the board swung down, his arm moved slightly to the side and the sound of a hard hit against the top of the box echoed through the building.

Feeling horror and anger, I knew that had the dog been hit, my cover would have been blown as I could not have remained indifferent. Realizing that the board was there for a purpose, I have no doubt that it had been used on this dog. The pup's cries were pitiful, and as I walked over I saw this mother dog flattened on the floor against the back of the box, trembling in terror and her eyes tightly closed. She did not look at me or make a sound. She did not move again while we were in that building.

As we were leaving, I noticed a tiny female miniature pinscher in a small cage placed away from the other dogs. A rear leg was at a weird angle. The miller said the dog had hurt her leg, but she was fine. I asked if a vet had checked her leg and he said no. This tiny girl trembled in silence. When the miller walked away, I reached thru the wire and softly touched her. This girl tugged at my heart.

The miller showed me shih tzus, Yorkies, and mixed puppies of all sizes and ages. He would bring out armloads of pups from an area I hadn't seen. They were covered with dried feces and fleas. As the miller held them, they never wiggled or moved but remained motionless with fear. The dogs rescued from this mill had no teeth, no lower jaws, broken jaws, broken bones. All were badly matted with feces-hardened hair. One little Pomeranian was so matted on his rear that he couldn't go to the bathroom. Some dogs have heartworm, intestinal worms, and some with medical problems that required surgery. Many lived with constant pain and no vet care. The millers do their own medical care to save money. People need to know that if they buy a dog from a pet store or a commercial Internet breeder, odds are

they are directly supporting this torture and misery. (From Prisonersofgreed.org.)

"The HSUS and You: Together We Can Abolish Puppy Mills"

STEPHANIE SHAIN, *Director of Outreach for Companion Animals, Humane Society of the United States*

As I sit down to write, dedicated staff from The Humane Society of the United States (HSUS) are on their way to help remove nearly one thousand dogs from a puppy mill in Hillsville, Virginia. This massive puppy-mill rescue—the largest in U.S. history—was led by local authorities who were spurred to act after being provided with footage from a five-month HSUS undercover investigation into Virginia puppy mills. One thousand dogs who this morning had nothing to hope for are about to realize today is their lucky day.

One thousand dogs. It's hard to even imagine what that looks like. In this case, you wouldn't readily see the dogs if you gazed at the property. You would see benign barns and sheds and rows and rows of cages . . . the kind of cages commonly referred to as "rabbit hutches," although we know that these cages are just as bad for rabbits as they are for dogs.

Get closer and you'd start to hear the barking . . . the unrelenting sound of highly social animals who are literally driven into madness because they are denied everything a dog needs mentally and physically.

Get closer and you'd start to notice the smell of urine and feces littered beneath the wire-bottomed cages—a smell these animals (with noses far more sensitive than ours) live over every day.

Get very close and you'd start to see the eyes peeking out at you. The eyes. Some are pleading, still craving the human attention they so desperately need; others won't hold your gaze, and look away and cower as you approach the cage; still others (the most heartbreaking ones) are those who seem not even to see you. They sit in their cage and don't react at all to anyone or anything that crosses in front of their cage door.

These dogs have been so broken by this abusive industry; they have been robbed of everything joyful that makes a dog a dog. It is difficult to see a dog suffer in any form. It is life-altering to see a dog whose very spirit has been broken. It is outrageous that the dog-loving public pays people to keep animals in conditions like this. Every penny someone pays for a puppy-mill puppy helps keep breeding dogs locked away, churning out litter after litter. Make no mistake . . . when someone thinks they "rescue" a dog from a pet store, they are putting another padlock on the cage door of that puppy's mother and father. The puppy mills can't survive without the full support of all those unwitting puppy buyers.

What Is a Puppy Mill?

One thousand dogs. One thousand is a huge number of animals, but is still just a drop in the bucket of the puppy-mill industry. The HSUS estimates that there are over 150,000 dogs kept as "breeders" in U.S. puppy mills at any given time. Each one is an individual whose barren life is an avoidable and unjustifiable tragedy. Those dogs produce 2–4 million puppies every year . . . puppies who will be sold through seemingly innocent neighborhood pet stores, fancy websites, and sometimes even through the local newspaper.

So what exactly *is* a "puppy mill"? The dictionary defines the term as "a commercial farming operation in which purebred dogs are raised in large numbers." That definition, while factually correct, doesn't come close to *really* defining the term. If it did, it would need to include a description of how the dogs live . . . in cages, for their lifetime. It would mention the constant breeding; the lack of attention to genetic problems; the disregard for inbreeding. There would have to be some mention of the typical problems with poor-quality food and dirty water, with the lack of veterinary care (even in the face of significant illness or injury). It would need somehow to give details of the burning smell of defecation, and of the temperature extremes dogs endure with primitive "shelter." It would be a definition that no one would ever want to read, and no one would believe such a place actually existed.

The bottom line, for anyone who cares about dogs, is that there are innocent dogs and puppies in U.S. puppy mills being kept in such horrific conditions that you'd fall down and weep if you saw it. And they wouldn't be there if it weren't for the public buying them. Puppy-buying dog lovers are a puppy mill's bread and butter.

The Sad History of Puppy Mills in the U.S.

Historically, we saw puppy mills in agricultural communities, where hundreds of barking dogs wouldn't be noticed by anyone. Today, we see an increase in "mini-mills" . . . operations with twenty to fifty dogs selling largely over the Internet and through newspaper classified ads. Make no mistake, while smaller in number, these operations keep dogs in equally poor conditions to their larger counterparts.

Puppy mills have been around for decades. Originally encouraged by the United States Department of Agriculture as a way for farmer's wives to make some extra money, they have grown into lucrative operations complete with lobbyists devoted to protecting the status quo of abusive treatment.

In 1970, the Animal Welfare Act was amended to include operations that bred dogs to be sold as pets. But the act only regulated businesses selling dogs wholesale, i.e., to pet stores—individuals selling directly to the public were not considered in the "business" of breeding and selling dogs, so their practices went largely unregulated. On one hand, few would argue that the government should inspect the homes of breeders who keep their dogs as part of the family. But on the other hand, the law has allowed thousands of large-scale breeding operations with hundreds of animals at each facility to grow and operate totally unregulated.

Regulations under the act cover minimum standards which must (in theory) be met. Minimum standards are just that . . . the bare minimum. They require that animals be given clean food and fresh water; they require that injured or sick animals be given veterinary care; and they require that the cages be of a certain size.

Imagine someone having to legally force you to give your dog veterinary care if his leg were broken? Or if he were so ill he couldn't even open his eyes, or chew his food because his teeth were so rotten and infected his very jawbone had started to disintegrate? When puppy mills are found with violations like this, they are not reported to local authorities for possible cruelty charges as you would be. Instead, they are given a report that notes their violation, and given a certain time period to "correct" it. Should the dog be gone when the inspector visits again there is no follow-up to find what happened to him or her to learn if he or she was given treatment or was simply allowed to suffer and die. (Puppy mills have been known to simply stop feeding sick or nonproducing dogs, allowing them to slowly starve to death.)

To be fair, the USDA has roughly one hundred inspectors at any given time. The inspectors are charged with inspecting over four thousand breeding operations in addition to zoos, circuses,

Some of the HSUS team: Jordan Crump (holding Murphy), Miyun Park (holding Yoda), Michael Markarian,
Wayne Pacelle (holding Baby), Stephanie Shain (holding Daisy), and Paul Shapiro.

and laboratories that use animals in their testing. That adds up
to over ten thousand facilities. It's not hard to see why
enforcement of the pathetically basic standards is so lax.
Remember this the next time you hear an industry apologist talk
about how strict "government oversight" is. Legislative efforts to
improve conditions for dogs in puppy mills are often fought by
groups focused on their "right" to do as they wish with their
"property" (the dogs). Additionally, groups like the American
Kennel Club (among others) have on more than one occasion
helped to torpedo state and federal legislation that would have
made life a bit better for dogs in puppy mills or shut down the
largest of the mills.

So What to Do about It All?

First: Educate! The Humane Society of the United States "Stop Puppy Mills" campaign has public education as its cornerstone. The book you hold in your hands is a wonderful example of public education. It is no accident that puppy mills exist in the shadows. Cute puppies rolling in the pet store window, photos of tiny pups surrounded by flowers or toys on a website, terms of endearment like "our little darlings" or "fur babies" all exist for one very simple reason: to fool the puppy buyer into believing that the puppy they are about to spend hundreds or thousands of dollars on came from a good place. Every effort is made to ensure there is no connection made between that cute puppy and the brutal existence his parents suffer under.

The only way we will end puppy mills for good is to dry up the demand for their "product" of abuse. So, whether by passing on a newspaper story, sponsoring a billboard advertisement, giving this book as a gift, or by simply telling a friend, we can all play a role in educating others about puppy mills. Help shine the bright light of truth on puppy mills by learning about them and then sharing that knowledge. When more people know about puppy mills and how to avoid them, we'll make a real dent in the puppy-mill owner's cash flow.

Second: Encourage everyone to adopt from their local shelter. One out of every four dogs in a shelter is a purebred. When people are adopting from shelters they can be certain they aren't supporting puppy mills. Rescue groups are another great choice, allowing you to find a specific breed. For people who want to buy a puppy from a breeder, direct them to our website (www.humanesociety.org/puppy) for tips on finding a good, compassionate breeder.

In the puppy-mill equation, the greatest victims are the parent dogs who suffer so greatly and for so long. Then, of course, there are the puppies. When a puppy is born into a puppy mill he or she faces a host of obstacles. Their health may be compromised long before birth, as their parents themselves are not always in top health. Add to that spending the first critical weeks of life devoid of human love and attention, being raised by a mom who is often so mentally damaged that her ability to mother suffers as well.

There are, however, another set of victims: the puppy buyers themselves. Puppy-mill puppies are more likely to suffer health and behavioral problems due to their bad beginnings. Common problems include intestinal parasites, pneumonia, the deadly disease Parvo, and a wide variety of genetic problems that vary by breed. Families bond with their new puppy instantly and suffer greatly when they must fight to keep their pup alive within days or weeks of bringing him home. The image of a new puppy under the Christmas tree is lovely, but a dying puppy two weeks later can ruin Christmases for years to come.

Third: Legislate! While the common refrain "Why can't we just ban puppy mills?" sounds simple enough (and glorious!), one look at the legislative efforts of puppy-mill fighters and you'll see it just isn't that simple. The puppy-mill industry fights every attempt to make even the smallest improvements in the dogs' conditions. For example, in 2007 there was an effort in Pennsylvania to require dogs be given twenty minutes a day outside of their cages for exercise. *Twenty minutes.* This, for dogs who will live their entire lives in cages. On the surface it sounds ridiculous, that out of the 1,440 minutes in a day animal advocates would fight for something as minor as twenty of those minutes to allow a dog to stand on solid ground, off of the mesh-bottomed cage they otherwise live on. Twenty minutes to be able to stretch their legs, to run, to roll around. The pet industry fought, and continues to fight today, against those twenty minutes outside the cage. While any sensible person could recognize that twenty minustes is not near enough, the pet industry argues that it is too much, that some dogs don't need that much exercise.

The HSUS works to pass laws at the state level to regulate large puppy-mill breeding operations to ensure that animals are at least being fed and provided with some sort of shelter. These laws are vitally important to improve the conditions for these animals in the immediate future while we work together diligently to teach others how to avoid puppy mills altogether. But these laws will linger, unpassed, if it is only animal welfare groups working for their passage. Without a groundswell of activity from individuals voicing their outrage over the systematic abuse that is allowed in U.S. puppy mills, legislative change will not come for these animals. While education will be the end of puppy mills, legislation will help us make the dogs' lives better in the meantime.

Fourth: Support! Whether it is the HSUS "Stop Puppy Mills" campaign, another puppy-mill action group, or your local animal shelter, support the work of animal welfare with dollars if you are able. The dozen shelters that stepped up to take dogs from that giant Virginia puppy mill wouldn't have been able to help had they not had ongoing and regular support from their communities. While shelters are saving lives every day, they are particularly necessary to help when a major case such as the Virginia one comes around. Had all their cages been full of unadopted dogs, had no one given them funds to keep in reserve, they would have had to say no when asked to help.

Some dogs like this book's heroine, Baby; those thousand Virginia dogs; and others who somehow, magically manage to get out of the puppy mill alive are the lucky survivors. We should

celebrate those victories and bask in the joy of them. But we must quickly turn back to the work at hand, because there are thousands upon thousands of dogs just as wonderful and deserving who sit without hope tonight in cages in puppy mills. We must all make a promise to them that we'll keep working to get them a lucky day when the cage doors open for good.

• • •

President Harry Truman once said, "If you want a friend in Washington, get a dog."

It was an astute commentary not only about politics, but also about the loyalty and devotion of our canine companions. That affection is returned by many members of Congress—from both sides of the aisle. Thankfully, the issue of animal welfare has become a concern to Democrats and Republicans alike, which makes me hopeful that new and stronger laws will be passed in every area where animal cruelty and suffering currently exist.

The members of the House and Senate who Baby and I met with

were visibly distressed to hear of the maltreatment she endured at a California puppy mill. More than one had tears in their eyes as they listened to the details of her abuse. At the time I wished I had brought a video camera to every photo shoot so that I could capture the outpouring of compassion and emotion. I needn't have worried—you can see it quite plainly in the photos; the tender, sad, loving, distressed, and compassionate faces of senators and congressmen who are anything but cynical when it comes to animal suffering.

Before our trip to D.C., I honestly didn't know what to expect from these meetings. After all, elected officials have countless numbers of people who pass through their doors on a daily basis, all of whom have various demands and concerns. It would not have been unreasonable for these politicians to be polite but perfunctory. And yet, the exact opposite occurred, which made their outrage over Baby's abuse and their pledge to stop it, all the more poignant.

Many of the members pictured on the following pages have taken strong leadership positions on a variety of animal-welfare issues by either sponsoring or cosponsoring numerous pieces of legislation. These men and women sponsor animal-welfare laws not because it's politically expedient but because they possess a deep-seated sense of mercy and compassion for the powerlessness and suffering of animals in our society. They deserve our gratitude for all they have done in the past and our encouragement so that they press on in the future and continue to be leaders in the fight against the inhumane treatment of animals—whether in the factory-farming industry or in the dog-breeding industry.

Those of us who champion animal-welfare reform have to be vigilant when it comes to those who lobby to maintain the status quo (the American Kennel Club among others). They claim to care for dogs and yet have opposed various animal-welfare reform legislation which would improve their condition. In the end we will prevail because we have truth on our side, namely the horrible evidence of abuse and cruelty at many of the commercial dog-breeding facilities.

If you'd like to know where your own senator or congressman stands on these issues, you can find out by visiting www.fund.org, which has a "Humane Scorecard" for all members of Congress. Fortunately, the animals have some terrific allies in Washington. The members featured here are but a fraction of those in Congress who are committed to supporting and advancing animal welfare legislation. Please call or e-mail them to thank them and cheer them on.

The "Dogacity" of Hope

Senator Barak Obama is an admirer of our sixteenth president, and so it was fitting that the Lincoln Memorial should be the backdrop for his portrait with Baby. Many people don't know that Abraham Lincoln was an animal lover who came to their aid on more than one occasion.

According to Lincoln's longtime law partner, there was an incident that took place in the winter of 1830, when the Lincolns moved from Indiana to Illinois. During the trip, one of their dogs fell behind. Once the family had crossed a prairie stream, they could see that the dog was left on the other side. Most of the people wanted to move on and leave the dog, but not Lincoln. In later life, when referring to the incident, he would say, "I could not endure the idea of abandoning even a dog. Pulling off shoes and socks I waded across the stream and triumphantly returned with the shivering animal under my arm. His frantic leaps of joy and other evidences of a dog's gratitude amply repaid me for all of the exposure I had undergone."

Baby and I first met Barack Obama in Chicago when he was running for the U.S. Senate. One day we went to his campaign office to talk to him about animal welfare issues. As we sat with him in a tiny office that could scarcely hold a round table and three chairs, he listened intently while I described Baby's ordeal. After sixty seconds in his presence, I remember saying to myself, *Not only is this man going to be the next senator of Illinois, one day he's going to be a contender for the presidency of the United States.* Barack Obama's intelligence, sincerity, and integrity—and, most important, his drive to see a more just and compassionate world—make for the most powerful and unforgettable combination, and I knew then that he was the real deal—someone who would play a pivotal role in our nation's history.

In the months following our meeting, I was delighted to receive e-mails from several people who had written to the newly elected senator, urging him to support a piece of animal welfare legislation that had recently been introduced. In his reply to them he mentioned having met Baby, and he pledged his commitment to stopping animal cruelty in all its forms. I was touched by the content of his letter and pleased to know that Baby had made it into official congressional correspondence.

And I believe that Abraham Lincoln was smiling down from above with wholehearted approval.

SENATOR BARACK OBAMA (D-Illinois)

SENATOR ELIZABETH DOLE (R-North Carolina) and LEADER

It is the seemingly little stories that people recall from childhood that are a window to their heart, such as the one told to me by Senator Dole when I asked her about her compassion for animals. I thought hers was among the most touching and beautiful anecdotes I had ever heard, and one that says so much about her capacity for empathy.

One can see from the photos of Senator Dole with Baby that this is a woman who still feels as deeply for the suffering of animals as she did when she was a little girl. Her own dog, Leader (the senator's husband, Bob Dole, was Senate Majority Leader), was intensely curious about Baby, wanting to know who the interloper was! Leader comes to the office regularly with the senator, as do several other congressional dogs. In a high-stress environment like the nation's capitol, it does the heart good to see that.

> 66 I have always had a deep love for animals and have experienced firsthand how much joy and companionship they can bring into our lives. I adored my childhood Chihuahuas, Penny and Peppy, who used to go to the kitchen each night to eat cheese with my dad, and Leader I and Leader II, miniature schnauzers, who've added richly to Bob's life and mine.
>
> "I'm told when I was little more than a toddler, my grandmother found me on the floor pulling back a corner of the rug. 'Elizabeth,' she asked, 'what are you doing?'
>
> " 'Oh,' I responded, 'I'm just hiding this little bug, because if Mother sees it, she'll kill it.' 99

Dennis and Elizabeth Kucinich have long understood the link between
compassionate treatment of animals and a more peaceful world.

SENATOR CARL LEVIN (D-Michigan)

66 A dog's ability to love without reservation or condition should be an example for us all. 99

SENATOR MARIA CANTWELL (D-Washington)

CONGRESSMAN SAM FARR (D-California),
CHIEF OF STAFF ROCHELLE DORNATT
and her dog, MAISEY

SENATOR DICK DURBIN (D-Illinois)

CONGRESSMAN ED WHITFIELD (R-Kentucky)

Congressman Ed Whitfield has been an important leader on animal issues, including the ban on horse slaughter. He was visibly pained to hear about Baby's ordeal and pledged to help put an end to puppy mills.

One of his favorite books on animal issues is *Dominion*, written by Matthew Scully, former speech writer for President George W. Bush. The congressman wanted me to include this passage from Scully's book.

Animals are a test of mankind's capacity for empathy and for decent, honorable conduct and faithful stewardship. We are called to treat them with kindness, not because they have rights or power or some claim to equality, but in a sense because they don't, because they all stand unequal and powerless before us. When we wince at the suffering of animals, that feeling speaks well of us, and those who dismiss love for our fellow creatures as mere sentimentality overlook an important part of our humanity.

SENATOR EDWARD KENNEDY (D-Massachusetts)

Senator Kennedy regularly brings his dogs to work. Notice the leash in his hand as he gets ready to take them for a quick stroll in the park across from the Senate.

FORMER SENATOR RICK SANTORUM (R-Pennsylvania) and CONGRESSMAN JIM GERLACH (R-Pennsylvania)

Both former Senator Santorum and Congressman Gerlach want to reform the dog-breeding industry, especially because Pennsylvania is one of the largest puppy-mill states, primarily in the Amish community. Santorum and Gerlach have worked to advance tougher laws, and both of these leaders have pledged to continue to fight for humane reforms at puppy mills.

SENATOR JOHN ENSIGN (R-Nevada)

Many people do not know that Senator Ensign was a veterinarian before being elected to the Senate. As a young boy he developed a strong sense of compassion for injured animals, which influenced his desire to heal them as a doctor. Since being elected to the Senate he's been a strong leader on numerous animal welfare issues.

As our trip to Washington came to an end, I wondered how long it would take for laws to be changed in order to protect animals from so many of the cruel and barbaric acts that we wage against them—such as being locked in a cage for their entire lives. I asked this question of lawyer and writer Steven Wise (author of *Rattling the Cage*, *Drawing the Line*, and *Though the Heavens May Fall*), who has been exploring the legal protection of animals for years, and he replied:

"Martin Luther King Jr. said that 'the moral arc of the universe is long, but it bends toward justice.' Because right-less creatures are invisible to judges and legislators, and nonhuman animals lack all rights, for centuries they have been treated as legal things that exist for the benefit of us legal persons, and not for themselves. Their interests have not counted.

"But this is just beginning to change, as our moral arc continues to bend. Human rights are becoming better protected, clever scientists are learning how complex are the minds of many nonhuman animals, and a rising worldwide animal rights movement is beginning to demand fundamental legal change. Sometimes sputtering, occasionally backsliding, this drive toward protecting the fundamental legal rights of nonhuman animals with such fundamental interests as not being imprisoned in cages or having their bodily integrity violated has marched forward. Judges and legislators are beginning to see them in a legal sense, to become more receptive to arguments that they have the right to live out their lives without our interference, and to be more willing to intervene to protect them.

"Those nonhuman animals who are the most mentally complex, the ones whose minds most resemble our minds, those who are most human-like—apes, dolphins and whales, elephants, and parrots—will be protected first through grants of legal personhood. But it will not stop there, and even those animals not initially given personhood—hens in battery cages, veal calves, dogs in puppy mills, and pigs in gestation crates—will be protected better than they are today."

Baby and I grab a quick smooch in the hall of a Senate office building before our next meeting.

The greatness of a nation and its moral progress can be judged by the way its animals are treated.

—Mahatma Gandhi

Chapter 5

When Laws Are Not Enough

If Gandhi was right, that our treatment of animals is a marker of our moral progress, then our country is in the dark ages. The brutality waged against animals in every animal-based industry is nothing short of barbaric. As essential as laws are to address that, laws are not enough to influence people's behavior.

We saw that in Chicago, after the foie gras ban was passed and some restaurants defied the law and continued to sell it or even give it away. This happened, in large part, because Chicago's mayor called it a "silly law." The mayor not only turned a blind eye to the violators, he gave them a wink and a nod with that remark. Many were outraged and ashamed to hear an elected official belittle an important anti-cruelty law and to ridicule animal abuse. His statement also insulted the legal systems of more than fourteen countries around the world—including Israel and Poland—who agreed that force-feeding was so cruel and inhumane, it must be outlawed. So, even with a law in place to protect animals, it isn't enough if there are those who will defy the law and leaders who will encourage them. That is where leaders from other parts of our society—such as family, school, and religious communities—are so desperately needed to influence our behavior.

For example, all of the major world religions have humane laws and edicts regarding animal welfare. Dating back to Moses, the ancient texts of Judaism make very clear that cruelty toward animals is in direct violation of God's express wishes and is a sign of an impaired moral character. Christianity, including the Bible, echoes these beliefs. This was not in reference to the aberrant torture of animals by mentally deranged individuals, but a directive toward how man and society should treat animals on a daily basis. Most of us have forgotten that the Third Commandment addresses the welfare of animals, namely that they should also receive a day of rest on the Sabbath: "Observe the Sabbath day and keep it holy, as the *Lord* your God commanded you. Six days you shall labor and do all your work. But the seventh day is a Sabbath to the *Lord* your God; you shall not do any work—you, or your son or your daughter . . . or your ox or your donkey, or any of your livestock."

In today's factory farming industry, not only are animals not given a day of rest, they are literally tortured twenty-four hours a day for years on end by being confined in cages where they cannot even turn around, then crowded into trucks and inhumanely transported for days on the road without food, water, or sleep, and finally slaughtered using methods that are anything but humane.

While in Los Angeles we came across this statue of St. Francis, the Patron Saint of Animals. Our hero!

Christianity and Animals

Jesus and St. Francis are noteworthy as Christianity's first animal-welfare advocates. So keenly aware was he of the interconnectedness of all living things that St. Francis referred to animals as his "brothers and sisters."

He forbade friars to chop down living trees, and he would pick worms off the firewood to keep them from being burned. . . . Once he traded his cloak for two lambs that were being hauled to the butcher and allowed them to live out their lives at the Portiuncula. One of these devoted sheep followed Francis everywhere.

—Robert F. Kennedy Jr.
Saint Francis of Assisi: A Life of Joy

And Jesus, of course, is depicted in the Bible as a gentle protector of helpless animals. Some scholars have pointed to historical evidence that may suggest Jesus, as a member of the Essenes, possibly practiced ethical vegetarianism. What would Jesus say if he were to see a puppy mill or a factory farm today?

Fortunately, there are increasing numbers of religious leaders in the Catholic and Jewish communities who are speaking out and reminding us that the Judeo-Christian ethic is steeped in humane treatment of animals. The current pope, Benedict XVI, issued one of the most compelling and magnificent statements on the matter of compassion toward animals

when he addressed the cruelty of factory farming. In 2005, in an interview in *God and the World* by Pete Seewald, then–Cardinal Ratzinger responded with compassion and insight when asked about his thoughts concerning the treatment of animals.

Animals, too, are God's creatures . . . creatures of His will, creatures we must respect as companions in Creation and as important elements in the Creation. We cannot just do whatever we want with them. Certainly, a sort of industrial use of creatures, so that geese are fed in such a way as to produce as large a liver as possible, or hens live so packed together that they become caricatures of birds, this degrading of living creatures to a commodity seems to me in fact to contradict the relationship of mutuality that comes across in the Bible.

Judaism and Animals

Rabbi Asher Lopatin is another religious leader who is setting an example by speaking out against practices that are inhumane in the raising and slaughtering of animals for food. In addition to adding his voice to the foie gras campaign, he has pledged to make the Jewish community aware of other inhumane food production practices, which are in conflict with the ethics and laws of Judaism. Rabbi Lopatin told me that the great Rav Kook of the previous century, the first chief rabbi of Palestine, believed strongly that the laws of kashrut (kosher dietary laws) were *all about* respect for animals and how to treat them properly.

      " While Judaism does permit the eating of meat, this concession to human desire—*ta'avah* as the Torah calls it—is severely limited through a host of laws of kashrut. Kashrut means that from the birth of the animal until its death the meat was prepared in a way that cares for the well-being of the life and death of the animal and respects the animal as a living being. These detailed laws require that animals be raised in ways which do not cause them any physical harm, known as the laws of *treifot*, that they are killed in a humane, painless way, the laws of *shechita*, and that even after slaughter the life of the animal is venerated by removing the blood from the meat. The blood is considered the life force—the *nefesh*—of the animal, and because Judaism wants us never to forget that we are eating what was once a dignified, living being, it prohibits blood in several cases. Even the choice of animals or birds or even organs are strictly limited in order to force human beings to limit their consumption of meat.

"In fact, the Talmud through later sources, notably Rav Avraham Yitzchak HaCohen Kook of the 20th century; strongly discourages eating meat, except for religious reasons, such as a holiday, or for special celebrations, such as a life-cycle event. The laws of kashrut—as well as other laws, such as rest on the Sabbath—demand a respectful attitude toward all creatures of God, and, if observed properly, should lead to treating all animals with care for their well-being. Three times a day a Jew is supposed to recite the verse from Psalms 145: God is good to all; God's mercy extends to all of God's creatures. Jewish law and custom has always understood that this verse applies to animals, and demands we imitate God in our kindness and humaneness. **99**

—*Rabbi Asher Lopatin*

Richard H. Schwartz, Ph.D., is the producer of the documentary *A Sacred Duty: Applying Jewish Values to Help Heal the World*

Q: Where does Judaism stand on treatment of animals?

A: Judaism forbids *tsa'ar ba'alei chayim*, inflicting unnecessary pain on animals. Most farm animals—including those raised for kosher consumers—are raised on factory farms where they live in cramped, confined spaces, and are often drugged, mutilated, and denied fresh air, sunlight, exercise, and any enjoyment of life, before they are slaughtered and eaten.

Q: As others are increasingly doing, you have drawn a connection between factory farming and global warming, and also world hunger. How is that?

A: While Judaism teaches that "the earth is the Lord's" (Psalm 24:1) and that we are to be God's partners and coworkers in preserving the world, modern intensive livestock agriculture contributes substantially to soil erosion and depletion, air and water pollution, overuse of chemical fertilizers and pesticides, the destruction of tropical rain forests and other habitats, global warming, and other environmental damage. A meat-based diet contributes more to global warming than all the cars, trucks, and planes worldwide. While Judaism mandates *bal tashchit,* that we are not to waste or unnecessarily destroy anything of value, and we are not to use more than is needed to accomplish a purpose, animal agriculture requires the wasteful use of grain, land, water, energy, and other resources.

As for world hunger, Judaism stresses that we are to assist the poor and share our bread with hungry people, yet over 70 percent of the grain grown in the United States is fed to animals destined for slaughter, while an estimated twenty million people worldwide die because of hunger and its effects each year. Judaism stresses that we must seek and pursue peace and that violence results from unjust conditions. Animal-centered diets, by wasting valuable resources, help to perpetuate the widespread hunger and poverty that eventually lead to instability and war.

Q: You also see a link between Judaism, diet, and health.

A: Judaism mandates that people should be very careful about preserving their health and their lives. Numerous scientific studies have linked animal-based diets directly to heart disease, stroke, many forms of cancer, and other chronic degenerative diseases.

In view of these important Jewish mandates to preserve human health, attend to the welfare of animals, protect the environment, conserve resources, help feed hungry people, and pursue peace, and since animal-centered diets violate and contradict each of these responsibilities, committed Jews (and others) should sharply reduce or eliminate their consumption of animal products.

No matter what our religious background is, we share a common belief in compassion and mercy toward animals. We have strayed very far from the ideals set down by our ancestors, but our present-day religious and spiritual leaders can use their influence to remind us of these sacred and holy commandments and beliefs, leading us back on the right—and righteous—path. Only then will we see more compassionate treatment of animals in every realm, and a more humane world for all.

Edward Grinnan, editor in chief of *Guideposts* magazine

As the editor-in-chief of *Guideposts*, Edward Grinnan may not be known by some, but for the millions who subscribe to that jewel of a publication, he's a beloved figure at the helm of something that is an anecdote to a stressful world.

Founded in 1945 by Dr. Norman Vincent Peale, who wrote *The Power of Positive Thinking, Guideposts* features stories of people who conquer life's obstacles with hope, love, and faith. They uplift you and make you feel closer to God and all of humanity. In my line of work, *that,* along with the people who make me laugh, are keys to my sanity.

Dr. Peale was also a minister at Marble Collegiate Church on Fifth Avenue in Manhattan. His widow, Ruth, a devoted partner to him for their long and happy union, turned 101 this year.

"I do not believe a person can be a true Christian and at the same time deliberately engage in cruel or inconsiderate treatment of animals."
—Dr. Norman Vincent Peale

Every month when I see my issue of *Guideposts* in the mail, I can't wait to curl up with it. I can't think of any magazine I've ever saved back copies of, but *Guideposts* and *Angels on Earth* (their other publication) are two I wouldn't dream of throwing away. I've saved every issue since I started subscribing more than ten years ago and will often re-read them whenever I need an extra dose of inner peace. Edward Grinnan's monthly letter and kindly face greet readers when they turn the cover. As I begin to read his simple yet profound message, I let go the worries of the day and of my challenging work.

"Heaven" by Edward Grinnan, Editor in Chief, Guideposts

THAT SATURDAY MORNING IN MAY, the first day of the year that had managed to fulfill the promise of spring, Sally wouldn't eat. My sixteen-year-old cocker had been declining all week, ever since my wife, Julee, had left for Germany for a series of concerts she couldn't reschedule. We'd talked about what to do if Sally worsened. "Do what's best for her," Julee said, climbing into the car that would take her to JFK and trying not to start crying again.

Actually Sally had been declining for some time, more than a year, refusing anything but baby food spoon-fed to her and needing to be carried outside. She walked like that old-man character of Arte Johnson's on the *Laugh-In* show, shuffling obstinately at her own pace amid the pitched pedestrian battle that is a New York City sidewalk. But you do those things for an old dog because there is nothing sweeter in the world.

I'd spent the last couple of days with Sally up at our house in the Berkshires of western Massachusetts because it was more peaceful there than in the city. Once Sally had loved to hike and climb and swim in these hills, and chase toads and butterflies in the yard. Now she spent almost all her time in her dog bed, which I positioned in a transient patch of sunlight then pulled across the living room as the day progressed, the warmth being good for her elderly bones.

That May morning I got down on the floor, lifted her head, and looked into her eyes. "Are you ready? Is that what you're trying to tell me?" It was time to do what was best for Sally, even if I didn't want to let go. I reached Julee at rehearsal in Cologne and held the phone to Sally's magnificent golden ear. Her eyes seemed to brighten. Then I lifted her up, carried her out to the jeep, and brought her to her vet's. Dr. Phillips said Sally's kidneys were shutting down and there was nothing more to be done. Except the kindest—and hardest—thing of all. The vet gave me a few minutes alone with my girl.

I watched her slow, shallow breathing. An image of a younger Sally came to mind, sitting on a heap of rocks at the top of our driveway, patient and alert, awaiting my return home. She knew my comings and goings intimately and was always in position, watching, waiting, even when I was late. It never felt like I was home until I saw Sally standing sentry. Why is it that we humans form such intense bonds with our animals? What makes us reach across the boundaries of species in search of something that, perhaps, we can't get from one another? Are we struggling to address some primal loneliness, an estrangement from our natural origins? How lonely this planet would be if we were the only creatures on it! How lonely it would seem without Sally.

"You are a good girl," I whispered, the ultimate canine compliment.

The shot was simple, almost routine, like so many other shots and vaccinations I'd held her for through the years, from puppyhood till now. I felt the weight and warmth of her as she let out a long last breath—a final sigh. And even in her old, sick body, I could immediately feel the manifest difference between living and not living, a kind of palpable lightness, as if the essence of who my dog was had left and gone somewhere else.

Where? I think heaven. If you are a doubter that animals go to heaven, I feel sorry for you. Either animals go there or no one goes there, because I cannot imagine a God who could contrive paradise without animals and the love and joy they bring us. What kind of a cruel heaven would that be? The fact that we can share the deepest and most complex emotions with our pets is proof. Only through the alchemy of two souls meeting can this kind of love take hold. And a soul lives beyond its mortal mantle. A soul belongs in heaven.

Which is why even today, as I build a bond with my new dog, Millie, that I know will last forever, I will stop and think of Sally chasing toads and butterflies, no more stiff hips or sore joints, no more pain.

There is nothing sweeter in the world.

Semillas de Amor Orphanage, Parramos, Chimaltenango, Guatemala

The reason I advocate for abused animals is because they're the lowest on the totem pole. They have no voice and no power to defend themselves. Of course I'm deeply concerned about any and all populations who suffer, including children.

With that in mind, one day I found myself reading about orphanages online and came across one in Guatemala called Semillas de Amor (Seeds of Love). The founder, Nancy Bailey, and I exchanged a few e-mails and even had a nice long-distance phone conversation, but my ever-increasing workload didn't allow me to travel there in person.

And yet, Nancy Baily's e-mails and the photos of the orphanage kept me connected. At one point I sent her a donation for the children and included some of the materials from this book to let her know a bit about my life and work. Her response took me by surprise and moved me to tears. I knew then that destiny had drawn us to each other.

"Sirius" by Nancy Baily

A LITTLE LESS THAN A MONTH AGO, my daughters and I were on a late afternoon walk with our three dogs (the mascots of Semillas de Amor). We were walking through a construction site when we heard crying. It was hard to see where it was coming from because of all the construction equipment. I finally found what seemed to be the site where the crying was coming from; a big shipping container.

I crawled under and I could see a silhouette of something very tiny. I stayed under the container and asked the kids to run up to the security gate and get a flashlight. The light was very dim, so I still could not quite see what it was that was crying so hard. But when I put my hand on the little body it stopped crying and began to whimper. It was then that I realized that the little body was tied up with fishing line and then tied to a piece of metal sticking out of the ground. I could not untie him so I sent the kids back to the security gate for a knife. I cut loose the baby and handed him to my daughter, Gaby. The baby was a tiny, less than a week-old, puppy.

His eyes were closed and he was cold. We rushed back home, set up my small walk-in closet as an intensive care unit, and went to work. Lots of sleepless nights later, the little puppy was doing well. We named him Sirius, after the brightest star in the sky from the Dog constellation. Now Semillas de Amor has one more mascot: little Sirius. Welcome, Sirius!

I can actually understand people's cruelty to each other more than I can to animals. Dogs are so very forgiving and full of love. I have always loved the quote, "I wish I could be the person my dog thinks I am." I often think that my dogs would make much better humans than I do.

Almost twelve years ago, my daughter, Gabriela, was given to me. She was four days old, weighed four pounds, and was dying. Nobody wanted to take responsibility for her. Like little Sirius, I took her home and kept her warm next to my body, fed her with an eyedropper, and never gave up on her. A few days later, she started to respond.

The issue that came up for me with Gabriela, Sirius, and every child that I have cared for in Guatemala is: If they can't defend themselves, then who will? Who will be the voice for those who don't have one? Whose responsibility is it to be that voice? When Gabriela was given to me, I had two sons—one was twenty-one and the other twenty-five. I was not interested in raising more children. But I also knew that if I did not take her in, she would end up in a government institution. I had every "good" reason not to take responsibility for her and speak on her behalf.

When I found Sirius, I had the same doubts. I already had four other dogs and didn't need another one, but I wondered, Who would be little Sirius's voice? Who would defend him? Often we don't take responsibility for those who cannot defend themselves, believing someone else will do it, or we just look the other way. I can't imagine my life without Gabriela. She has enriched my life in so many ways and made me a better person. And the joy of watching little Sirius blossom and grow has given us all such delight. I believe that when you take a risk, and take responsibility, your life changes. It may not be the life you thought you would have, but being a voice and standing up for beings who cannot speak for or defend themselves, you have an honor bestowed upon you by the Universe that will make you the person you are *meant* to be.

Gaby and I talked about "her story" the night we found Sirius. I told her about "paying it forward," and that even though she was giving something back by taking in Sirius, I knew it was not the last time that she would be saving a living being.

by Gabriela Bailey, age 11½

We found an abandoned puppy that was born around the thirteenth of August. We found him on the sixteenth of August. My mom and I took care of him by keeping him warm and feeding him baby formula with a syringe. When we found him, his eyes and ears were closed, but now they are open. We blend puppy food with baby formula and water for him—he also drinks water from a bowl. He plays a lot, and we decided to name him Sirius, after the star. Because of Sirius, I learned that not only ourselves matter, but other animals do, too. Also, if you find an abandoned or wounded animal and you take care of them, it feels great when you look into their eyes and see that look that says, "Thank you!"

Thank you, Sirius, my teacher, my companion, and my puppy.

Gabriela Baily and Sirius on the day of his rescue.

Why We Are Mean

Mean is a word that children use. "She's so mean!" or "You're being mean!" we often hear them say. Yet that's the word that comes to mind because the reason we are, in fact, capable of being cruel (as the grown-ups say), or indifferent to cruelty, is rooted in our earliest years and is the result of something most of us have suffered to one degree or another—narcissistic injury.

"Not me!" you say. I'm a caring, compassionate person who didn't suffer any kind of emotional injury, narcissistic or otherwise. I wouldn't think of hurting a child, an animal, or any helpless creature.

Perhaps not in the way you are accustomed to thinking of cruelty. We may not be guilty of inflicting pain with our own hands—such as those who torture dogs to goad them into fighting, or the veal farmer who takes baby calves from their grieving mothers and chains their necks to crates so they cannot even turn around, or the dog breeder who imprisons dogs in cages for their entire lives—but if we are told about such acts and do nothing to stop them, or continue to support such practices through our buying habits, are we not guilty of indifference to cruelty, and so are we not cruel? Consider the following:

I remember describing to an acquaintance several years ago what I had just learned about fur production. As someone who owned furs myself, I was in an ideal position to raise the issue with her. I described the horror I had seen in videos about fur farming, the unspeakable torture I saw with my own eyes—all for the sake of a status symbol or a strip of trim on a sweater. I felt compelled to tell her and others in my circle who, like me, had been wearing fur not knowing how it was produced. Her reply was chilling and, needless to say, gave me serious pause in terms of building a closer friendship. After hearing the gruesome description of anal electrocution and steel leghold traps that require an animal to chew off its own limb in order to escape, she said, "Well, I love animals, too, but I don't love them that much. I mean, not enough to give up fur!"

I was stunned. Here was a woman I didn't know well, but she and her husband were a smart and successful couple, both professionals, who would balk at the notion that they were lacking in compassion or were cruel. They would have cited that they gave generously to charities and sat on the board of worthy causes. And yet, her indifference to the torture and suffering that I had described was due exactly to the kind of insidious narcissistic injury that is the scourge of our world. Selective empathy, I call it. This woman was capable of great empathy when the cause or charity pertained to her own ethnic or self-interest group, but she was amazingly cold toward the suffering of those she deemed beneath her or outside her circle of concern.

How does selective empathy occur in someone who is otherwise a decent person? Dr. Alice Miller, a psychoanalyst and writer who I greatly admire, has explained it better than anyone I know. In her book *For Your Own Good: Hidden Cruelty in Child-Rearing and the Roots of Violence*, she provides insight into the question of why even seemingly decent people may be cruel and/or indifferent to cruelty. In short, the subtle (and not-so-subtle) ways that parents may dismiss a child's feelings result in the narcissistic wounding of a budding psyche, leading to an adulthood marked by indifference to cruelty for some of us, and outright cruelty for others. That child harbors those wounds on an unconscious level, producing devastating consequences, not only for himself but for his loved ones and for society. The narcissistic injuries of our formative years inform many of the problems that we face as a people and a planet—from mental illness like depression and anxiety, interpersonal struggles such as those reflected in our high divorce rate, child abuse, oppression of women and minorities, crime, poverty, world hunger, global warming, aggression toward other nations, and, of course, the exploitation and abuse of animals in every animal-based industry.

Each of those ills can be traced back to the original intolerance of a child's feelings and needs, which get played out in that individual's adult life and then exponentially in the lives of millions of other wounded adults, creating wounded societies and a wounded world. What results is a narcissistically wounded country, religion, or race exploiting and injuring another whenever and wherever it can as a result of early emotional wounds that were never healed. So powerful is the unconscious drive to reenact the original drama that we will do so even to the point of self-destruction, as in the case of humans exploiting the Earth to the brink of our own demise and that of scores of species that we will never see again. Our pathological need to exploit and abuse has extended even to the very resources that sustain our life and survival on Earth.

But it's too deliciously tempting for the narcissistically injured adult to *not* do this. The vulnerable and easily exploited—animals, children, women, minorities, the poor—are low-hanging fruit we cannot resist. For the once-powerless child who is now an adult and at last in a position to exert some power of his own, how can he resist? With our unconscious driving us, we are urged to reenact the original hurt, whether it was a violent parent-child power struggle in the extreme, or the subtle yet contemptuous expressions or silences a well-meaning parent may have used in response to our weaknesses, which served as an uncomfortable reminder of the parent's own weaknesses that his own parents (our grandparents) could not tolerate.

A wounded psyche that has never been allowed to mourn its original injury must reenact it again and again against others who are weaker. This is an unconscious compulsion, with the individual now in the role of the aggressor and dominator instead of the helpless victim. If mourning of the original injury never takes place, healing cannot occur, and if healing doesn't occur, the oppression of others will be carried out—whether in the guise of a greedy corporation, who, like an insatiable child, seeks to own and dominate everything in its grasp even at the risk of exploiting others (the poor, the environment, its own workers, animals) or the well-meaning but emotionally withholding parent whose love and approval are conditional, based on a child's ability to echo and mirror that parent's own narcissistic needs. Even well-meaning

When children are treated with compassion and mercy, they extend that to other living creatures. Those who abuse animals, whether legally in animal-based industries or illegally, are likely to have been raised to ignore suffering in others as well as in oneself.

parents may unknowingly be guilty of unconscious payback for the way they themselves were treated as children.

At one time there may have been a seemingly rational reason for parents to try to "toughen up" their children as a means of surviving a cut-throat environment or society, but many of those threats are gone, and the defense mechanisms that were created to avoid vulnerability are no longer necessary or relevant. In fact, many of those defense mechanisms, such as denial of emotional pain or intellectualization of others' pain, typically make children more susceptible to failure on a personal or professional level, and sometimes both, and do great harm to our collective society. It is not just the Hitlers, Stalins, and Mussolinis of the world who embody this phenomenon, based on the similarity of their abusive childhoods; it is those among us whose unhealed childhood wounds also wreck havoc upon the world—such as the millions who enabled Hitler to carry out his plan. As Alice Miller points out, without them the Holocaust would never have happened. A well-known German doctor of a previous generation, whose child-rearing manual was a staple in every home in the late 1800's, encouraged an entire population to use the harshest methods imaginable to train children, including beating infants and toddlers. The fate of the doctor's own two sons did not bode well for his methods: One committed suicide and the other developed psychosis. Miller believes that the entire German nation was doomed by such brutal and abusive child-rearing techniques.

The range of ills caused by narcissistic injury run the gamut, from extreme cases to those of us who are, for all intents and purposes, decent people but who nevertheless are dulled in our capacity to experience our truest selves; whose ability to feel compassion is stifled, and who are therefore inclined to be indifferent or even unconsciously contemptuous of the neediness or suffering of those beneath us on the ladder of power, including animals.

Another scenario that may also produce indifference to animal suffering concerns grandiosity. Someone may report that she was not emotionally discounted by her parents at all and had, in fact, been elevated by them. But this, too, can have the effect of narcissistic injury if a child is not simultaneously encouraged to show empathy toward the plight of others. Unconditional love is one thing, but if it occurs in the absence of empathy for others, it becomes an ideal training ground for a cold and indifferent heart. In fact, our grandiose sense of place in the world as the "superior" species is the reason our world is in such a perilous ecological state.

If we lock our dog in a crate all day while we are away, or use a medieval choke or pinch collar on his neck that serves to break his spirit during our walks with him, are we not being indifferent to the suffering of a fellow creature? (We must try these collars on our own necks and give them a good yank, if we think they're not so bad). We convince ourselves that it is for the dog's own good, or that it's necessary in order to evoke good behavior, but we're kidding ourselves. It is more about our need to control and exert power over someone or something weaker, just as we were once weak and powerless under an authority who was indifferent to our suffering. Dog trainers Tamar Geller and Victoria Stilwell have demonstrated that love and positive reinforcement are all that is needed to elicit good behavior from our dogs, not punitive methods that say more about our vain attempts to gain control over ghosts from our past.

If we buy a bird as a pet, lock it in a cage, and deprive it of its wondrous gift of flight, all the while claiming to love it, where is our empathy for that creature's needs? It is buried so deep in our own injured narcissism that it does not even occur to us how incredibly cruel it is for a winged creature—or any living being—to be imprisoned in a cage. We can access only our own needs—namely, that we find the bird beautiful to look at or that his sweet song is lovely to listen to, and we want to have it as a pet. We are incapable of even putting ourselves in the position of the bird, who was meant to live his life outside, flying from tree to tree and soaring the open skies. We would balk at anyone who calls us cruel for keeping our bird in a cage. We love our bird. We gave him a name. We feed him good seed and fresh vegetables. We even let him out of the cage sometimes so he can fly a few feet from one end of the room to another.

So how do we go from *mean* to *nice?* One way is for our society as a whole to take steps to ensure that we raise emotionally healthier citizens. A crucial first step would be to outlaw corporal punishment of children, as they have in Sweden, Denmark, Norway, and Finland. It's no coincidence that those countries have fewer incidents of interpersonal violence than we do, which may explain why nearly all the rest of the European nations have decided to follow suit.

But emotional injury will need to be equally addressed. We must also begin to look at ways we can heal those adults who are long past the childhood stage; the walking wounded who inflict their suffering upon others, and who, unfortunately, sometimes occupy important leadership roles in politics, religion, or pop culture. Only then will the vulnerable—children, animals, women, even our environment—be safe from those who are exploitive. Only then will we begin to see a healthier, happier country and peace between nations.

No matter how slight the childhood injuries, we must mourn them in order to release the hold they have on us. Only then will we be able to see the world through empathic eyes and not be inclined to inflict our injuries upon others. When individuals are *not* physically or emotionally wounded, they navigate through life quite differently than their wounded counterparts; they are not unconsciously driven to seize opportunities to exploit others. Rather, these individuals see how those who are weaker and more vulnerable may be affected by their actions, and they are able to monitor themselves accordingly. Furthermore, they have come to understand on an intellectual as well as an emotional and a spiritual level that by not inflicting pain they elevate their own self-esteem and personal worth. They know that every act of kindness or mercy they perform in the service of those who are more vulnerable is an affirmation of the original child in all of us who needed—and still needs—respect, compassion, and nurturance. Even the smallest act of benevolence over cruelty—or over *indifference to cruelty*—is an advertisement to the world of where we're at in terms of healing those early wounds.

Not only does our collective psyche take a beating when we mistreat animals, but we are now seeing a multitude of other ways that we suffer because of our abusive ways. For instance, we now know, according to data released by the United Nations and another study from the University of Chicago, that livestock farming contributes more to global warming than all the world's trucks, cars, and planes combined; that foie gras has been shown to produce proteins implicated in arthritis, Alzheimer's, diabetes, and tuberculosis; that the inhumane confinement systems used at poultry farms (battery cages) result in the unsanitary conditions that produce avian bird flu; and that the chemicals and drugs pumped into factory-farmed animals, necessary in order to keep them alive in the brutal conditions that they must endure—not to mention the stress chemicals the animals themselves produce as a result of being tortured—are ingested by us when we eat them, all of which are implicated in a host of diseases, including cancer.

In short, what hurts the animals hurts us.

And all of it is being done in the service of our unhealed wounds, for who could possibly engage in any of the above acts and be an empathic person? It takes a dulling of the mind and spirit to carry out such acts and be able to overlook the fact that the caged animals who are crying and flailing about as they wait to be slaughtered are sentient beings who suffer and feel pain, too. All because we haven't mourned the original injury to our own spirit when we were helpless, powerless little beings ourselves.

It is only when we undertake an in-depth exploration of how and why we lack empathy, and employ a plan of prevention, that we will be able to enjoy a safer world for ourselves and our children. It will require that we take a hard look at the way we live, our values, and most of all the emotional pain that some of us carry deep within, which we have never given voice to or allowed to surface, let alone heal. That deadly essence spreads when left unchecked, manifesting itself in an ever-more violent world, or one in which too many of us are coolly indifferent to the suffering of those who have no voice and no power. If we should choose to embark on a journey of individual and collective self-examination, the rewards could be monumental, with the potential to change the world.

It isn't easy for any of us to contemplate the possibility that we grow up thinking we are decent, law-abiding people, never considering the ways that we may be mean. But if we return to the original source of injury and mourn those early wounds, even those we may have thought—or been told by others—should not have bothered us, we have the chance to not only be released from the past, but to enjoy more fully the present. Most important, we will be less likely to hurt others, and more likely to allow them to live as they were meant to live.

All it takes for evil to prevail
is for good men to do nothing.

—Edmund Burke

Chapter 6

Coming Together

When I considered the best way to raise awareness about puppy mills, celebrities naturally came to mind. They sell magazines, books, and products. They're the source of much of our entertainment and often an escape from the harsh reality of our world and our sometimes hum-drum lives. We love watching them, reading about them, and hearing what they have to say. One of the things I didn't expect to discover about celebrities is that they're just like you and me, with the same worries and hopes we all share.

One important difference, however, that gave me a newfound appreciation for the challenges they face, is that they're asked to do a million things. Yes, I know that you're pulled in a million directions in your own busy life, perhaps juggling the endless demands of family and career, but the difference is that they have the added pressure of having to do everything in the public eye. They can't sneeze without it being reported to the world. Every move they make is tracked and scrutinized. Everyone wants a piece of them—their fans, the press, work, charitable groups—all hoping for and expecting something. Of course, it isn't humanely possible to fulfill every request, and so they have to say *no* a lot more often than *yes,* which risks disappointing the very fans they rely upon.

And they aren't allowed to keep it real. If you or I are in a bad mood for whatever reason, or if we look like hell on a particular day, we don't have to worry about putting up a false front. But if a celebrity goes out of the house looking like a mess, or if they're in a grumpy mood for a perfectly good reason, the press is all over them—making fun of them, criticizing them, or sometimes going so far as to fabricate a story just to sell a paper. Imagine being ridiculed or misrepresented in front of millions of people. It would make me want to be a recluse. Which is exactly what some of them are. And who can blame them?

All of that makes me especially grateful to the celebrated men and women who posed for this book. They are the nicest of people that I've had the honor to meet, with the biggest, most compassionate hearts and a genuine desire to use their status to make the world a better place. The animals are lucky to have them in their corner.

Psst! Were we supposed to go tinkle before we got on the plane? *A generous donor heard of Baby's plight and offered to give us a ride on a private plane to the photo shoots. This was not only a special treat, it was a necessity. Baby can't fly commercially because she can't be put in a carrier as mandated by commercial airlines— after years of being locked in a cage, she gets physically ill when put in a confined space.*

Baby at her first hotel. Between room service and the big, fluffy bed, not to mention having me to snuggle up to, she was one happy pooch during our first night together.

"Ma" loved the idea of going camping, but when she thought about the spiders, snakes, bears, and mountain lions, it didn't sound like so much fun. Instead we went to the North Face store and "camped" there for an hour.

So many firsts, including smelling the roses near our hotel and soaking up the healing rays of the sun.

JAMES CROMWELL
Actor

James Cromwell was the very first celebrity I approached for the book. I had seen him at a benefit for HSUS and was so impressed by the remarks he made when he received an award that night. He was humble, intelligent, sensitive toward the suffering of animals, and a man of vision who had keen insight about the world. Jamie, as his friends call him, is completely unpretentious and warm when you meet him. When he agreed on the spot to do a photo shoot with Baby after hearing about the project, I was so excited to have our first celebrity on board, I practically jumped up and down like a kid. At that point the project was only a dream, and Jamie made it a reality by giving me the first yes.

In this shot he looks like a giant next to Baby. In my mind he *is* a giant of a man.

66 In 1973, I rode across country on my motorcycle. Somewhere, in the middle of Texas, the road went through an enormous feedlot that seemed to go on for miles. Pens packed with terrified animals lined the road on either side as far as the eye could see. Wild-eyed and frantic, they bellowed their despair to the vast emptiness that engulfed us. The din, the stench, the horror overwhelmed me, and I wept with them.

"That experience began a journey. The choice I made during the filming of *Babe* was that I could no longer countenance the egregious cruelty and suffering inflicted on animals: the factory farm, fur farm, puppy mill, gestation crate, battery cage, drift net, bush meat, horse meat, foie gras, bear bile, bull fighting, dog fighting, cock fighting carnage, all the myriad ways we abuse, exploit, and consume other sentient beings. You've only to hold Baby in your arms to feel the love and the trust animals bestow on us, as well as the cost they pay for our ignorance and unconscious savagery. We cannot be human and countenance such horror. All life is sacred. 99

JUDGE JUDITH SHEINDLIN
Presiding judge, *Judge Judy*, author, with rescue dogs Zorra, Happy, Lulu, Roscoe, Jasper, Reggie, Pico, Billy Bean, Tatum, and Baby

The title of one of Judge Judy's best-selling books, *Don't Pee on My Leg and Tell Me It's Raining,* says it all about her. Almost. What you might not know is that while she may be tough as nails, she's also very soft spoken and kind. And obviously sexy!

At the photo shoot we were so star struck. One of my friends, a neurosurgeon, even drove up from San Diego just to meet her. It was a riot. All of these rescue dogs on the bed with her, and the dog moms nervously hoping their "kids" would sit still and behave for the Judge.

I had read all of her books before the shoot and brought them with me for her to sign. When I saw what she had inscribed, "To Jana—A good person and my friend . . . Judy," I thought, if my house were ever on fire, I'd have to grab that.

Q: How did you become concerned about animal welfare?

A: *Finding an abandoned and malnourished puppy some forty years ago. It's only a small step from animal abuse to people abuse.*

Q: What have you learned from sharing your life with animals?

A: *You always get more unconditional love than you give.*

Q: What would the public be surprised to see or hear that you do when you are alone with your dogs?

A: *I cook for my babies—beg them for kisses—and spoil them rotten.*

Q: If a puppy mill owner were standing before you in your courtroom on charges of animal cruelty, what would you say to him or her? What do you think is a just and appropriate sentence for such crimes?

A: *I would say that there must be a special place in hell reserved for people who torture animals. Until you get there, you'll deal with me.*

LORRI BAUSTON
Cofounder of Farm Sanctuary in Watkins Glen, New York, and founder of Animal Acres, in Acton, California

Notice that these turkeys had the end of their beaks cut off by the farmer they were rescued from, which was to prevent the birds from pecking one another, a natural response to being overcrowded. Turkeys raised for meat are genetically engineered to double in size every week. The goal is to manipulate the animals' bodies so that they grow as fast as possible in the shortest amount of time to maximize profits. In the end, the birds cannot even walk because their breasts have grown too heavy, a result of the farmer trying to increase production of white meat. The turkeys seen here were seized by humane officers after being discovered in squalid conditions.

These goats and sheep, so scared after their ordeal, were even afraid of Baby and me when we entered the barn. They had been seized by humane officers when they were discovered in grisly living conditions at a farm. Emaciated and weak from malnourishment and dehydration when they arrived, they required daily veterinary treatments, but are now thriving at Animal Acres Sanctuary.

But this little piglet named Jamie (as in Cromwell!) didn't seem to worry about us. Jamie was rescued by humane investigators from a California stockyard after he was abandoned and left to die. He was only two weeks old, but already a victim of the cruel factory-farming industry. His mother had given birth to him and his littermates while she was at the stockyard, and then she was sold for slaughter. Unfortunately, piglets like Jamie who are born at the stockyard are considered worthless and are discarded as though they are garbage. The stockyard workers left Jamie and the other piglets to fend for themselves, and they would have starved to death. When they came to Animal Acres, Jamie and the two other piglets, named Charlotte and Jorja, were near death. After proper care, they have grown into happy, healthy pigs who spend their day roaming the hills of Animal Acres with the other sanctuary residents. The most treasured part of their day, however, is when visitors spoil them with belly rubs and treats.

66 The link between violence toward animals and violence among humans has long been known: Perpetrators of violent crime commonly abuse animals before they graduate to human victims. But even the 'legal' kind of abuse and violence toward animals, namely that which occurs in livestock farming, has been shown to result in greater violence among humans. Gail Eisnitz's book *Slaughterhouse* recounts the shocking and disturbing testimonies of slaughterhouse workers whose daily job of killing animals in the brutal fashion that is standard in the food industry, led them to acts of violence against their wives, children and members of their communities.

"One slaughterhouse worker said: 'I've had ideas of hanging my foreman upside down on the line and sticking him [killing him]. I remember going to the office and telling the personnel man I have no problem pulling the trigger on a person—if you get in my face I'll blow you away. Every sticker I know carries a gun, and every one of them would shoot you. Most stickers I know have been arrested for assault. A lot of them have problems with alcohol. They have to drink, they have no other way of killing live, kicking animals all day long.'

"Animal Acres is a place where a lucky few who are rescued come to live in peace, and see for the first time that humans can be kind, not violent. **99**

—Lorri Bauston

HEATHER MILLS
Humanitarian, with Baby and "Lucy" Piatek

Traveling to New York for Heather's photo shoot, our plane had a mechanical problem and the pilot told us we'd have to stop in Ohio to change planes. This would make us more than two hours late to the shoot, and I was nervous about calling Heather. Being late to any appointment is bad form, especially when someone is doing you a huge favor. Plus, I had never met Heather and didn't know how she might react.

I dialed her number from the Ohio airport, bracing myself for maybe an irritated assistant or secretary, but I was about to learn that Heather is quite comfortable handling many things herself that others in her position might delegate. She answered the phone herself, and when I told her the situation, she cheerfully and thoughtfully replied, "Oh, I'm so sorry. But don't worry at all about me. I have plenty to do here. When you get here, you get here. Please don't worry. Just relax." I hung up and thought, *That's a very nice person.* In fact, when we got there, she worried about how tired we must be and offered to have us stay overnight in the country with her instead of driving back into the city.

When I learned how cruel the press was to her, I was sickened. Heather is as nice and decent a person as they come, and the only explanation I can come up with for the bad press is that sometimes people have the urge to create a good versus evil dynamic, which psychologists call "splitting." I believe that must be the case with some journalists. I believe that Heather will have the last word, though, because her good deeds speak louder than anything else.

Whatever charitable mission she has undertaken—whether helping victims of land mines, or animals who are abused—she has done so with integrity and always in the service of others. Some people's lives are meant to be dedicated to helping those who have no voice—and they are destined to work for the betterment of mankind. Heather Mills is one of those people.

As Baby and Heather are both amputees, I asked her about phantom pain and if there was any advice she could give to make Baby more comfortable. She asked if I massaged Baby's amputation site and I said no. I massaged her existing front leg because I figured it was fatigued from putting all her weight on it. I actually avoided touching the amputation site because I didn't know if it would feel painful or irritating to her. Heather explained that it was the contrary, and that it would probably feel wonderful to Baby to have it massaged, so now I give that area plenty of TLC.

You've come a long way, Lucy! From trash to treasure, this little angel is now a cherished member of my friend Wendy Piatek's family in Indiana. I insisted that Wendy and Lucy come to the shoot with Heather because they both deserve to be recognized. A puppy-mill owner had put Lucy and thirty other "spent" breeding dogs (too old to produce litters) in boxes and thrown them away. After the dogs were found and put into the local shelter, Wendy, one of the greatest animal advocates and philanthropists I know, gave Lucy a home. Wendy, who is also working to abolish puppy mills, has about eighteen special-needs rescue dogs; some are blind, others crippled. Lucy's heart is too big for her chest cavity and her front legs are maimed, but the quality of her life is still good and she revels in the love she finally found in Wendy's home. Since the writing of this book, I'm sorry to report that Lucy has passed. I join Wendy in mourning the loss of Lucy, who suffered for years at the hands of dog breeders, but whose last days were marked by love.

MATT TOLMACH
President of production, Columbia Pictures,
Thalberg Building Screening Room

66 After my parents divorced, my father moved from Washington, DC, to rural Maryland, and quickly assimilated into the local culture. All of it. Pickup trucks, fishing, county fairs, dirt bikes, and hunting. Raccoon hunting.

"Before long, we had five coon-hounds. I'd visit on weekends, and Dad and I would spend long nights slogging through the woods as our hounds hunted, their beautiful voices echoing through the dark hollows. We loved the dogs. And although they weren't terribly good at getting the job done, occasionally they'd run a raccoon up a tree.

"And then we'd shoot it down.

"This went on for a few years. We became part of the local scene. Sometimes we'd go out hunting with the fellas from up the road, whose dogs were much better trained than ours. And on those nights, many more raccoons died.

"One night, as we stood around the base of a tree, our bright lights shining up into the face of a trembling raccoon, my father slowly turned to me— almost like he'd been lost—and said, 'What are we doing?' And I understood the question. We'd both been lost, father and son.

"And that was the last time we ever hunted. We didn't talk about it. We just collected our dogs and went home for good.

"Our hunting dogs quickly became just our dogs. They slept at night and went on long walks in the woods. And they died old and happy.

"But I'll never forget. I'm haunted by it.

"I'll fight for animals for the rest of my life. I love my dogs like I love my child. My wife rescues squirrels and birds and anything that needs us. But somehow I know that I got here because of what happened in the woods. **9 9**

MONTEL WILLIAMS
Talk show host

Montel, as everyone who watches him knows, is one of the most compassionate people anywhere, and animal cruelty is something that pains him deeply. I remember once I attended a benefit for HSUS and he was the master of ceremonies. He spoke about various forms of animal abuse with such distress and outrage that people in the audience were moved to tears. From that instant, I knew I wanted him to be in the book. When we met at his studio, he was as lovely as can be, as was his staff, which is always the case.

❝ Every religion has a tenet that has to do with how we treat those who are the 'least' of us. Just the thought of animal cruelty brings me to tears when I look at my beloved dog, Max, and I wonder how these things could possibly happen in our society. ❞

MARTINA NAVRATILOVA
Tennis legend and humanitarian

Meeting Martina Navratilova was big for me, but discovering that the cause closest to her heart is helping animals was even bigger.

Like everyone else in the world, I'm in awe of Martina, having spent years watching her win one championship after another, achieving what no other athlete had in the history of the game (since my own mother was the U.S. Indoor Champion in 1954 and '57, I grew up in a tennis family, so I couldn't help but be awe-struck by Martina's accomplishments).

To learn that one of her primary missions is to help homeless animals find their forever homes, and that she has come to a place in her life where she prefers the company of those who are like-minded, was a wonderful revelation.

Before we took this shot with two of her rescue dogs, Athena and Baby (yes, another one!), she talked to me about how important this issue is to her.

Q: How did you develop this empathy and compassion for animals?

A: *I always loved animals. I always wanted a dog and a cat but I didn't get a dog until I was fifteen. I just can't imagine not having compassion for animals.*

Q: A lot of people may say they like animals, but they don't necessarily go out of their way to help them, as you do.

A: *Well, my friends do. I think you sort people out in terms of who you want to hang out with or not by how they react to animals in need. If they're not interested, then I'm not interested in them. So it's a great parameter for what kind of person I think you are, because if you don't have compassion for animals, you certainly cannot have compassion for people. You cannot just separate the two.*

66 For decades, freshman medical students here were instructed to vivisect—that is, cut up while alive and then kill—fifty to sixty dogs per year in their physiology and pharmacology courses. Since I practice medicine as well as teach, I knew that this annual slaughter of the innocents was completely unnecessary in physician education, and circulated a petition signed by hundreds of other San Diego doctors asking UCSD to stop it.

"When they refused, I conducted and published a nationwide survey that showed that 95 percent of U.S. medical schools taught pharmacology without killing any animals, let alone dogs, and 82 percent of physiology courses were similarly cruelty-free. But UCSD kept killing dogs. I next petitioned the University's Animal Welfare Committee to stop the dog labs, but their Orwellian newspeak response was that lifelong caging, vivisection, and killing dogs raised 'no animal welfare issues.'

"Resorting at last to an appeal to the public, dozens of San Diego physicians and local animal advocates staged a protest, held a press conference, and I did television interviews on Dog-Killing Day in 2002 to draw attention to the issue. The resulting very negative publicity worked where appeals to reason and compassion had not. Finally, feeling the heat after refusing to see the light, the unnecessary dog-vivisection labs in physiology and pharmacology at UCSD were ended in 2003. 99

LINDSAY LOHAN
Actress

When Lindsay made her way down the impossibly long press line at the *Georgia Rule* premiere, her publicist, Leslie Sloan, and Marie Griffin, the publicist who helped with celebrity outreach for this book, told her who Baby was, since we had sent them Baby's story in advance. I recounted Baby's ordeal and when Lindsay took her from me and saw her missing limb and heard about her vocal cords being cut, her red-carpet smile dissolved. She was utterly distraught, and I remember thinking what a kindhearted person she must be. I've told Baby's story to more people than I can count, and that kind of instinctive reaction told me that Lindsay is someone with a beautiful, tender heart.

JANE FONDA
Actress, activist, author

66 Abusers have usually been victims themselves at some point. They can heal from this. I have seen it. Often it's by working in group therapy with former abusers who have become counselors. The most successful healing programs are those that view violence and abuse through a gender lens. When women and girls have been abused, they take it inside themselves. It manifests as depression, inability to trust and connect intimately with others, and often promiscuity. Male abuse victims tend to act out with violence—against animals or women—or other men. Their abuse has caused them shame. Their manhood—their identity—is threatened and they strike out as a way to regain their manhood. This is what patriarchal culture does to men: It creates a definition of manhood that is so vulnerable to shaming that it must constantly be shored up through violence. We need to work with men to change the very definition of manhood. 99

The appointment to photograph Bill Maher sent Ma into a tizzy. That morning she had her hair washed and blow-dried at the hotel salon, had her nails done (all four paws!), and then proceeded to try on everything in her closet—twice!

I wanted to say, *Hey! I'm the one being photographed—not you!* Ma apologized for acting so silly, explaining that she was his biggest fan. *Everyone thinks they're his biggest fan,* I wanted to tell her. *Come on, let's get a move on before he changes his mind.*

Bill turned to mush when he held me. Only moments before, he had been talking to his staff about something, and I could sense from across the room how tense he was, but the instant he took me in his arms, his face, his body, his very energy completely changed. As he listened to Ma describe what happened to me, he kept whispering in my ear, "I'm sorry. I'm so sorry."

Everyone in the room got very quiet. Ma later told me she got choked up and had to bite the inside of her cheek so she wouldn't cry. To see such a soft, tender side of him moved her deeply.

66 The animals are the most innocent, most speechless, most defenseless creatures, and they deserve a mean, take-no-prisoners, son-of-a-bitch like me talking for them. 99

A musician doesn't let just anyone stand on his guitar!

The talented singer-songwriter-guitarist (who is also a big animal advocate) was inspired by Baby to write a beautiful and uplifting collection of songs especially for this project. (You can order the CD from www.RareBreedofLove.com.)

JAY McCARROLL
Designer, winner of *Project Runway*, Season One

As many know from watching *Project Runway*, Jay is hilariously funny and entertaining. When I met him in person for this shot, I could have listened to him for hours. But he's also a person of depth and substance. That's why I wasn't surprised to learn that he's a cruelty-free designer (look closely at the pin he wore that day). When Jay was in design school, he made the decision not to design with fur.

> 66 It's not like we are Inuits living in igloos. I wish more people would see wearing fur for what it really is . . . a murdered animal hanging off your back. There is nothing luxurious about it. It's gross. Cruel. And unnecessary. 99

In a folder marked "E-mails to save forever" there is a message from Alice Walker that I received after having sent her the invitation to be included in this project. She thanked me for doing this book, telling me how important she thought it was, which meant the world to me.

"The animals of the world exist for their own reasons.
They were not made for humans any more than
black people were made for whites or women for men."

—ALICE WALKER

Crimes Against Dog

MY DOG, MARLEY, was named after the late music shaman, Bob Marley. I never saw or heard him while he was alive, but once I heard his music, everything about him—his voice, his trancelike, holy dancing on stage, his leonine dreadlocks—went straight to my heart. He modeled such devotion to the well-being of humanity that his caring inspired the world; I felt a more sincere individual had probably never lived. Considering his whole life a prayer, and his singing the purest offering, I wanted to say his name every day with admiration and love. Marley has grown up on his music; Bob, leaning on his guitar in a large poster on my living room wall, is regularly pointed out to her as her Spirit Dad.

Marley was born on December 19, 1995. She shares a birth sign, Sagittarius, with my mother and several friends and acquaintances. At times I feel surrounded by Sages and enjoy them very much: They are fun to be with, outspoken, passionate, and won't hesitate to try new things. They also like chicken. Marley has all these qualities, though I didn't know that the morning I drove out to the breeder to look at the litter of Labrador retrievers I was told had arrived.

Crossing the Golden Gate Bridge, a friend and I joked about whether I was in fact ready to settle down enough to have a dog. Who would feed it when I was distracted by work? Where would it stay while I was away on book tours? Had I lined up a reliable vet? I had no idea what would happen. I knew only that this friend was about to go away on a journey of unknown length. I would be unbearably lonely for her. I needed a companion on whom to lavish my overflowing, if at times distractible, affection. I needed a dog.

My first thoughts are always about enslavement on entering a place where animals are bred. Force. Captivity. I looked at the black and chocolate labs who were Marley's parents and felt sad for them. They looked healthy enough, but who knew if left to themselves, they would choose to have litter after litter of offspring? I wondered how painful it was to part with each litter. I spoke to both parents, let them sniff my hand. Take in the quality of my being. I asked permission to look at their young. The mother moved a little away from her brood, all crawling over her blindly, feeling for a teat; the father actually looked rather proud. My friend joked about offering him a cigar.

I was proud of myself, too, standing there preparing to choose. In the "old" days of several months before, if I were going to choose an animal from a litter, I would have been drawn to the one that seemed the most bumbling, the most clueless, the most unamused. I saw a couple like that. But on this day, that old switch was not thrown: I realized I was sick of my attraction to the confused. My eyes moved on. They all looked much alike, to tell the truth. From a chocolate mother and a black father there were twelve puppies, six chocolate, six black. I'll never get over this. Why were there none with spots?

I asked the woman selling them, whom I tried not to have slave-trader thoughts about. She shrugged. "They never spot," she said. That's the nature of the purebred Lab. *Well,* I thought. *Mother. Once again doing it just any old way you like.* "Mother" is my favorite name for Nature, God, All-ness.

I settled on a frisky black puppy who seemed to know where she was going—toward a plump middle teat!—and was small enough to fit in my hand. I sometimes wish I had chosen a chocolate puppy; in the Northern California summers, the dust wouldn't show as much, but I think about this mostly when Marley rolls in the dirt in an effort to get cool.

After seven weeks, I returned alone to pick her up, bereft that my friend had already gone on the road. It didn't feel right to pay money for a living being; I would have been happier working out some sort of exchange. I paid, though, and put Marley in my colorful African market basket before stroking the faces of her wistful-looking parents one last time. In the car, I placed the basket in the front seat next to me. I put on Bob Marley's *Exodus* CD, and baby Marley and I sped away from Babylon.

We wound our way back through the winter countryside toward the Golden Gate Bridge and the bracing air of San Francisco. Before we had gone twenty miles, Marley, now about the size of my two fists, had climbed out of the basket and into my lap. From my lap she began journeying up my stomach to my chest. By the time we approached the bridge, she'd discovered my dreadlocks and began climbing them. As we rolled into the city she had climbed all the way to the back of my neck and settled herself there between my neck and the headrest. Once there she snoozed.

Of the weeks of training I remember little. Dashing down three flights of stairs in the middle of the night to let her pee outside under the stars. Sitting on a cushion in the kitchen, before dawn, her precious black body in my lap, groggily caressing her after her morning feed. Walking with her zipped up in my parka around and around the park that was opposite our house. Crossing the Golden Gate Bridge on foot, her warm body snug in my arms as I swooned into the view. She grew.

Dogs understand something I was late learning: When we are mean to anyone or any being it is because we are temporarily not ourselves.

Today she is seven years old and weighs almost ninety pounds. People we encounter on walks always ask whether she's pregnant. No, I reply, she's just fat. But is she really? No matter how carefully I feed her or how often I downsize her meals, she remains large and heavy. And she loves to eat so much that when her rations are diminished she begs, which I can't stand. This is one of those areas that we've had most work to do. I've settled it lately by taking her off any slimming diet whatsoever and giving her enough food so that she seems satisfied. I did this after she was diagnosed with breast cancer, had surgery, and I realized I might lose her at any time. I did not want her last days to be spent looking pleadingly at me for an extra morsel of bread. To make up for giving her more food, I resolved to walk her more.

The friend who went away never really returned. Marley and I ceased expecting to see her after about the first year. Marley was an amazing comfort to me. What is it about dogs? I think what I most appreciate in Marley is how swiftly she forgives me. Anything. Was I cool and snooty when I got up this morning? Did I neglect to greet her when I came in from a disturbing movie? Was I a little short on the foodstuffs and forgot to give her a cube of dried liver? Well. And what about that walk we didn't take and the swim we didn't have, and why don't I play ball with her the way I did all last week? And who is this strange person I want her to go off with? It doesn't matter what it is, what crime against Dog I have committed, she always forgives me. She doesn't even appear to think about it. One minute she's noting my odd behavior, the next, if I make a move toward her, she's licking my hand. As if to say: *Gosh, I'm so glad you're yourself again, and you're back!*

Dogs understand something I was late learning: When we are mean to anyone or any being it is because we are temporarily not ourselves. We're somebody else inhabiting these bodies we think of as us. They recognize this. *Oops,* I imagine Marley saying to herself, sniffing my anger, disappointment, or distraction. *My mommy's not in there at the moment. I'll just wait until she gets back.* I've begun to feel this way more than a little myself. Which is to say, Marley is teaching me how to be more self-forgiving. Sometimes I will say something that hurts a friend's feelings. I will be miserable and almost want to do away with myself. Then I'll think: But that wasn't really the you that protects and loves this friend so much you would never hurt them. That was a you that slipped in because you are sad and depressed about other things: the state of your love life, your health, or the fate of the planet. The you that loves your friend is back now. Welcome her home. Be gentle with her. Tell her you understand. Lick her hand.

From left to right: Apollo, Noelle, Athena, Baby, Benny with Baby (that's right—still another Baby!)

MARIA MENOUNOS
TV personality and reporter

Animal cruelty is an issue that's close to Maria's heart. She has done exposés on puppy mills for the *Today Show* and has rescued dogs herself. Her five precious pups live the good life now and all were so welcoming of Baby. Even with five dogs to care for, Maria told me about another dog she had seen at a local shelter who desperately needed a home, and she was considering going back for him the next day. I came away from the shoot thinking she was one of the nicest, most compassionate people I'd met.

"When I was a child and most other girls had posters of rock stars on their walls, I had pictures of animals instead. I love them and have always had a strong connection with them."

KIMORA LEE SIMMONS
Model, designer, entrepreneur

Kimora is the tallest woman I've ever met, but don't think gawky—she is the epitome of feminine elegance. She looked like a queen at her Baby Phat runway show, and her two adorable daughters, who were also there wearing the sweetest party dresses, looked like princesses. Holding Baby, Kimora knelt down and quietly explained to them exactly what had happened to Baby—that someone had abused her, which is why her leg was amputated, and her vocal cords cut. I remember how touched I was by her compassion and impressed that she had told her girls the truth about what happened to Baby. They were riveted to her every word and gently reached out to pet Baby.

At one point during the shoot, Kimora clutched Baby to her chest and said, "Can she come live with me?"

After we left Kimora, we headed back to the hotel. It had been a hot, sticky day in Manhattan (which is worse than a hot, sticky day almost anywhere else), and Baby and I were pooped. I could hardly wait to take a bath and collapse into bed. In my haste to get up to our room, I almost knocked a man over as I entered the hotel lobby, and as I turned to apologize, he had already passed me, but I could see that it was none other than Steven Tyler. I had almost run over the lead singer of Aerosmith!

I mumbled "I'm so sorry," as we all got into the elevator and he offered me and Baby the nicest smile. You know how sometimes in a millisecond you can read someone? Well, in that instant, as I looked at his face, I knew he was a really nice guy. My fatigue, of course, was now replaced by racing thoughts of how to invite him to be in the book, realizing I had only a few floors to give my spiel. And so I did, and by the time we had gotten to his floor, he said, "I'd love to take a picture with Baby. Come to the room in about a half-hour and we can do it before I have to leave again for a show."

As it happened, one of the people with him in the elevator was a professional photographer, Gitte Meldgaard. My mouth agape at our incredible luck, I giddily pranced back to our own room (amazing how I went from feeling like I could hardly put one foot in front of the other to practically doing cartwheels down the hall). For the next twenty-five minutes I didn't take my eyes off the clock, so nervous was I about being on time. What if he changes his mind? What if leaves before we get there and we miss him?

Thirty minutes later, on the dot, I rang the bell to his room and practically sighed out loud when we were warmly welcomed into his suite by his security and Gitte, who proceeded to take these photos of Steven and Baby with a pocket-size digital camera. She apologized for not having her regular camera and equipment with her, but I wouldn't have cared if she had used a disposable drugstore camera. I was so incredibly grateful to them both for this gift. We stayed for a few minutes, talking to them and the others who were there—everyone wanted to hear Baby's story—and then floated back to our room.

I would say that that ranked as one of the most exciting experiences I've had on this project. I had never met a rock star before, and not only did I get to meet one of the all-time greatest, but I got to see firsthand that he's a terrifically nice guy.

AURÉLIA THIÉRRÉE
Performer

Aurélia has an amazing lineage as the granddaughter of Charlie Chaplin and the great-granddaughter of Eugene O'Neill. She is in her own right a talented performer who travels the world putting on shows that combine elements of dance, circus, and drama—in many ways a combination of the art forms associated with her legendary relatives. At one time she and her parents used animals in their show, but, she is glad to report, no longer.

Aurélia is half French, half English and she speaks with a beautiful accent, which filled my head as I read her story. She has the look and carriage of many French women—elegant, refined, pulled together without even trying. I usually feel like a clod next to women like that, but Aurélia's humility and kindness are refreshingly disarming.

❝ My mother was getting ready to go on stage the night I was born. Summertime, they had a circus then. Until they broke away from it and created a new kind of circus, with no animals, just the four of us.

"I ran away from it all when I was fourteen. I wanted to live in a house, go to school, meet teenagers. But I kept coming back. As an adult, I started missing it. I started missing the scent of the theater. Wood. The dressing rooms. The silence of a stage before show. And my family. I went back. A show directed and created by my mother. It is what I know and love.

"I like the theater because it is about repetition. I am obsessed with repetition, and yet it is never the same. The elusive pursuit of moments. The infinite possibilities within those moments. The intensity it provides. Suddenly, one night, you realize there is a different way of saying something, of doing a move, and it clicks into something so logical and revelatory that it makes you feel alive and content for a little bit.

"We traveled with rabbits and ducks who had their own dressing rooms. I grew up with them. Each spring, we found baby crows who fell from their nests, and we raised them until the fall, when they flew away.

"One day there was Louis, a bird whose species could not be identified, not even by the vet who vaccinated him. My father found Louis in Valencia, Spain. A man was giving him away. Louis was in a very bad state; his cage was small and dirty and at first it looked like he wouldn't pull through. But he did. It took about a year. He stayed with us for eighteen.

"We discovered a creature with a personality so strong, he became a center to our lives. His moods, annoyances, desires were impossible to ignore. His gaze could break your heart. He was a small bird, probably from Africa. A few times, he slept outside, mostly in the countryside. In the early morning, we'd call his name in anguish until in the distance, far away, a lone chirp would resonate. Then a dot would appear, grow, followed by the sound of his flight crescendo, and finally the *thump* of his body landing nearby, cheerful, happy.

"Sometimes he flew into your bedroom, onto your bed, and leaned so close to your face, his beak would brush against your nose, his eye staring into yours with insistence, probably looking at his own reflection in your retinas.

"He was a bee hunter, he went into elaborate, dramatic choreographies each time he caught one.

"We can only assume that he died of old age, for he was close to twenty. But who knows what species he was, really, and if he wouldn't have lived for another sixty years? 🙰

Eric and his wife, Tania, are big animal lovers who support various causes. Like many others I'd met on this project, I was in awe of his great talent. *Monty Python. Spamalot.* We took this shot on the Broadway stage of *Spamalot,* and I kept saying to myself, *Somebody pinch me.* At one point, the cast and crew gathered around to hear about Baby and offered to help as an ensemble, by doing a public service announcement or whatever we needed. It was an unforgettable shoot. When I saw the show that night, I was mesmerized from beginning to end by how clever Eric is.

Beth is not just the fiancée of legendary radio host Howard Stern, she's also a big-hearted animal advocate whom I adore and admire. The sweetness you see in this picture is 100 percent genuine. Lucky for Howard and lucky for the critters she's determined to help!

Q: Why is animal rescue and adoption so important that you decided to become a spokesperson for The North Shore Animal League?

A: *I've been passionate about animal rescue my entire life. My parents adopted our childhood pets only from local shelters and instilled in us the importance of rescuing, nurturing, and adopting homeless dogs and cats. When North Shore Animal League America witnessed my devotion and love for their mission, they asked me to be a spokesperson. I'm honored to have had the privilege to spread the word of their incredible work!*

Q: Does Howard share your compassion for animals in need?

A: *I am so lucky that my fiancé, Howard, is just as passionate in helping and rescuing animals. We are actively involved not only in North Shore Animal League America, but in the Long Island English Bulldog Rescue and the Hamptons Wildlife Rescue. I love that he lets me use his show as a vehicle to inform others and ask for help for animals in need. We have a fifty-four-pound English bulldog, Bianca Romijn-Stamos (named after the two most beautiful people in the world who happen to be our friends!), who is the love of our lives! Howard has his own special relationship with Bianca. Whenever she sees him, she immediately rolls on her back to get her belly rubbed. They have their special summer-beach-morning walks together on which I am not invited!*

Q: What is the most endearing trait of your dog, Bianca Romijn-Stamos?

A: *Bianca is never in a hurry, therefore it makes us slow down and appreciate every little thing in our daily lives!*

Maggie, the show's resident dog, stood so still for the shot that she looks like one of the props on Jim's desk.

JIM CRAMER
Host, CNBC's *Mad Money*

Even as a boy, Jim Cramer made millions on paper when he studied the market. The brilliant Harvard law school grad has now become one of the world's most successful investors and trusted financial advisors. But as you'll read in his autobiography, *Confessions of a Street Addict,* Jim was homeless for a time, living out of his car, which might explain his compassion for strays. When we met, I was as impressed with his kindness as his brilliance—and the people who work with him are equally big-hearted. The trickle-down theory of kindness in action!

> 66 My kids can't bear to see any animal be hurt. That's why we take in cat after cat after cat who would otherwise be put to sleep, which is a lot of strays these days. Whether it be Happy or Buddy or Fang or Nemo or Iverson or the late and much missed Dinah, Cousy, Bessie, Flo, Big Foot, and Lucky, strays are the joys of our kids' lives. Now, if only Starsheema would come back, our last stray, who hopefully found a new home! 99

PERSIA WHITE
Actress

"" My pup's name is Kisses Le Rough Williams White. She is a rescue that was found in the desert. I later learned that the desert is a place where people dump unwanted dogs. A friend on the set of my television show, *Girlfriends*, who works in animal rescue, knew about Kisses and was searching for a home for her. I fell in love with her the moment I looked into her eyes. ""

GLORIA STEINEM
Activist, author

Gloria has always been a role model for me, as she has for millions of women, and I especially admire that her sense of justice naturally extends to all groups who are oppressed. She's one of those rare people who is both a visionary and a great leader. What you aren't prepared for when you meet her is that she has a very gentle demeanor. I've had the good fortune to spend time with her, which has been an extraordinary experience. To get to know a living legend up close and personal and to discover that along with being wise she is also wonderfully kind, has been an inspiration.

"Moji"
by Gloria Steinem

IN MY CHILDHOOD, the animals we loved and lived with were never purchased—they just happened into our lives—like falling in love. Perhaps a family's dog or cat had given birth, and good homes had to be found for the offspring. Or perhaps my new shoes for Easter came with a free baby rabbit. Or perhaps my dog had puppies that I couldn't bear to part with, and we had six or seven grown dogs before I could give away even one.

Now that I know about the terrors of commercial puppy mills and the many animals awaiting adoption in shelters, I would be even less likely to buy a living thing. But there is another reward for letting animals come into our lives however they will: Each one arrives with a story.

Moji, the dog you see here, has lived not just a story but a novel. David Bale, who moved here from South Africa and England in 1991, found him as a puppy running in the streets of East Los Angeles. His paws were bloody and his skinny body was infested and dirty, but he had the good sense to trust David enough to get into his car and fall asleep. Gradually, Moji became a part of the Bale household that included a big dog rescued from a sadistic owner, several stray cats, and the occasional injured bird or possum.

Moji especially loved David's teenage son Christian, and, despite Moji's street-dog penchant for running off for a while, or going through the garbage when he was alone and feared being abandoned again, they became devoted companions. Since Christian was an admired young actor, Moji also acquired press clippings and even a following on the Internet.

In 2000, when Christian married and left home, Moji became David's companion. When David and I married later that same year, he became my dog, too, and often flew with us as we commuted between Los Angeles and New York. We thought of writing a book about his adventurous, starvation-to-steak life, with chapters like "Moji Rides in a Plane!" and "Moji Goes to Central Park!"

Of course, there was still sadness in him. One could see it in his fear of small children, or his growling at men in boots. By such patterns of fear, animals tell us who abused them.

But Moji looked for us out the window when we were gone, and raced up and down with joy when we came home. He came with us to restaurants because David always opted for the outdoor ones where dogs were welcome, and we found hotels that included doggy dinners with room service and even registered Moji as a guest.

After two years or so when David became ill, I can only guess what Moji felt as his rescuer weakened, disappeared for many months into hospitals where dogs were not allowed, and then was so changed by brain cancer that, when Moji finally could visit him in a nursing home, I'm not sure that they even knew each other.

Since David's death at the very end of 2003, Moji and I have been each other's companion. He loves all the smells and sights and the dog life of the streets of Manhattan, and often attracts admiring comments with his charming blend of Jack Russell markings and beagle size. Of course, he and I are most proud that he is a dog with street smarts in both Los Angeles and New York.

In 2005, a big stray cat of about eight or so joined us. He appeared in the woods near the New Jersey house of a friend of mine, and she nursed this dirty and bedraggled creature back to health. She also tried hard to find his original home, but was unsuccessful; perhaps just as well, since someone had declawed him, a cruel practice that's now beginning to be outlawed. I sometimes wonder if that was why he ran away.

Because my friend has twenty or so rescued cats around her country house, life was hard for this big clawless new arrival that she called Galahad. He needed to live in a one-cat household. With regret at losing his loving and even-tempered company, she brought him to live with us. After contemplating each other for a month or so, Galahad and Moji decided all was fine. Indeed, Galahad looks so self-satisfied as he sprawls purring on my desk, that I wonder if he wouldn't rather be called Chessie, after the smiling Cheshire Cat from *Alice in Wonderland.*

Clearly, the oldest cultures were right when they spoke of the two-legged and the four-legged, the feathered and the finned as "all our relations." Living creatures were not meant to own each other, but to share our worlds.

Sure, Jane has an audience of millions who watch her on television, but can she do this?

JANE VELEZ-MITCHELL
Journalist, author

66 I wrote the book *Secrets Can Be Murder: What America's Most Sensational Crimes Tell Us About Ourselves,* to encourage Americans to look beyond crime and punishment and focus more on violence prevention. Through education and therapy, our society can and must begin to intercept violence before it becomes homicidal.

"As a journalist, I have witnessed many gruesome crimes. I am always stunned by how self-destructive violence is. It invariably destroys not just the victim but the perpetrator as well. Violence is irrational and senseless. Its seeds are sown at a young age. It often starts with cruelty to animals and works up from there. We also have to look at the everyday violence that we law-abiding citizens commit. Most Americans start their day by killing. The victim is on their plate. The consumers who subsidize horrific cruelty to animals on factory farms are the accessories and coconspirators to that crime. There's a saying I really love: Peace Begins on Your Plate! Check out the concept. If everyone refrained from killing animals, we might become incapable of killing one another. That's why I am a vegan. 99

KEVIN NEALON
Comedian

There's an old saying that those who know how to make people laugh automatically earn a place in Heaven. In my line of work, being surrounded by people who can do that is key.

When Kevin heard about Baby's book, he invited us to come to one of his shows, but they were all sold out. He told Mike Lacey, the owner of the Comedy and Magic Club in Hermosa Beach, "Baby deserves some laughs." Mike agreed and not only squeezed in an extra table, he put us in the front row!

JILLIAN BARBERIE
Television host

66 The fact that I was adopted played a huge role in my rescuing animals. I was saved from whatever evils were out there in the world by the family who adopted me, and subconsciously I am doing the same with my rescues. Teddy was a rescue from my show (I introduced "Adopt a Pet" twelve years ago). He was found tied to a fence and was terrified of children. He had fleas and mange, but when I saw his face, I knew instantly that he was mine. I still bring him on the show to encourage people to adopt. He gets more fan mail than the show can handle! Today Teddy has come so far that he even loves kids.

"Samba was found in a Dumpster and was also up for adoption on our show. It was Valentine's Day and she had a huge Valentine's Day card pinned to her collar that said, "Please give me a home . . . nobody loves me." Well that was it for me! She didn't ever make it on the show because, like Teddy, I took her home. She has her separation anxiety issues but is happy and knows I would never ever abandon her. **99**

GENE BAUR
Cofounder and president, Farm Sanctuary,
Watkins Glen, New York, and author

Farm Sanctuary, along with The Humane Society of the United States, was one of the groups I worked with on the foie gras campaign. Gene has worked for years to protect farm animals from the abuse that is standard in factory farming. He is a soft-spoken, gentle person who I have learned much from, and the author of *Farm Sanctuary: Changing Hearts and Minds About Animals and Food.*

"Kohl, Harper, and Burton are the innocent victims of the foie gras industry. Kohl came to us unable to walk or stand. He was in respiratory distress, and after weeks of force feeding could not eat on his own. He was taken to Cornell University Hospital for Animals for urgent care. In the intensive care unit, he was put on emergency oxygen and intravenous fluids. Upon testing, it was confirmed that his liver was abnormally enlarged and that he was suffering from hepatic lipidosis (fatty-liver syndrome or liver disease). The gross enlargement of his liver had decreased the air space for his lungs and caused his respiratory ailments. Due to his abuse and neglect, his legs are also severely deformed. He will never walk or swim like a normal duck.

"Harper arrived in our care missing his left eye. He was having difficulty breathing, and his head tilted abnormally. The left side of his head was malformed and depressed more than the right. His potassium and uric acid levels were low as a result of the protein-deficient diet fed to foie gras ducks. Further adding to his struggle, his bill was deformed.

"Burton arrived at Farm Sanctuary stumbling. He had an enlarged liver and severe mucus in his upper respiratory tract. Along with Kohl and Harper, he had to be tube-fed formula because he could not eat on his own.

"Kohl, Harper, and Burton suffered through one of the worst kinds of torture on earth. But they have escaped from the foie gras industry to see a different side of humanity at Farm Sanctuary. Here they are beginning to trust that they will be cared for with a loving touch each day. Thankfully, they will now forever know human hands as reaching out to help, rather than hurt them. Unfortunately, because of the cruel treatment that Kohl, Harper, and Burton endured at the hands of the foie gras industry, they will be debilitated for life."

Right before this shoot, I had read in John's autobiography, *Tears of Rage*, about the tragic murder of his son, Adam. Of course, I was already familiar with the events, but the book provided the details. When we met, I just wanted to throw my arms around him and sob. I told him that I had just finished the book, and I muttered something about how I felt and he nodded, no doubt having heard the same from countless people he has met over the years who have the urge to cry with him about what happened.

John is undoubtedly one of the most extraordinary people I've ever had the honor to meet. The way he has lived his life since that tragic day is nothing short of astounding. He's a testament to the power of the human spirit and the will of one man to change the world. Just look at the child-protection laws that he has single-handedly created. He's as powerful an example of what one person can do as I have ever seen. With that in mind, I wanted to invite him to be in the book, sensing that he would have a strong sense of protection for helpless animals who are abused. When he met Baby and heard the details of her abuse he was outraged, as I imagined he would be.

❝ I believe in justice—for *all*. **❞**

WE DON'T RENT PIGS!

NOAH WYLE, Actor

Noah Wyle and his family share their idyllic mountain home with abused and abandoned animals—dogs, goats, chickens, horses, and pigs like Hamilton, who came from a rescue group called Little Orphan Hammies. The sign on his house tells visitors "Our pigs are here to relax, not work," he explained.

"Hamilton is house trained—uses the bathroom outside and then comes in to curl up for a good movie," says Noah's wife, Tracy. "Pigs are incredibly smart. People are surprised to find that they're among the smartest animals on Earth, ranked even higher than dogs on intelligence and sensitivity scales. That makes the torture they endure at hog farms, where they're locked in crates for years and unable to even turn around, all the more unbearable."

BRIDGET MARQUARDT
Costar of *The Girls Next Door*

" Growing up in an apartment in Northern California, there were no animals allowed. But when I was nine, my mom remarried and we moved to the country. Jeff, my stepdad, had seven acres of land with cows, horses, two dogs, and two cats. I quickly fell in love with the animals, spending time brushing the horses, petting the cows, chasing the kitties, and lounging with the dogs.

"My new school offered a program called 4-H. I was excited to join and chose a rabbit to raise. She was a black Netherlands dwarf rabbit and I named her Hershey Kiss, Kissie for short.

"Years later, I dreamt of getting a black Persian kitten for an in-house pet. My parents were not keen on having animals in the house, but then I found the perfect kitty. Her name was Gizmo and she quickly became my baby. My parents fell in love with her, and when it was time for me to move out and Gizmo came with me, they missed her terribly. I wanted to get them a kitten to replace the void that Gizmo and I had left in their lives, and this led to my first experience with a commercial cat mill. The cats were matted and unhealthy. They were all contained in cages that lined the walls, the smell was terrible and the overall feel was disheartening. I did not buy a cat from that mill but continued looking. I finally found a family that had kittens they were raising in their front room with hands-on love and care, which is where we purchased the kitty for my parents.

"Gizmo has been through a lot of life changes with me, and she is always there to snuggle or make me feel better. She has experienced many moves, met a lot of people, and traveled with me. Somehow she always seems to know when people are sad and need a little kitty love. It is like she has kitty intuition, and even though she is fairly independent, when she sees that someone needs a little extra love, she will go and lie beside them.

"When I moved into the Playboy mansion, there were, and still are, tons of animals here—birds, monkeys, and, of course, a lot of dogs! Gizmo is the only kitty at the mansion. It is very much a dog's world here, but Gizzy is holding her own.

"After being at the mansion for a few years and seeing everybody with their sweet dogs, I began to long for that companionship. Gizmo and I are close and have a wonderful relationship, but she is independent and self-sufficient, and I had much more love I wanted to give. I tried to see if Gizmo wanted to run errands or go on walks, but she clearly was not interested and preferred staying home sleeping on her tree. I decided I wanted a dog that looked like my kitty, and that's when I found Wednesday, a black miniature Pekingese. She and Gizmo have become the loves of my life. Between the two of them, they make my life complete.

"Life with Wednesday has been amazing, and our relationship continues to blossom. She really keeps me grounded and reminds me to appreciate the simple things. At times it can be pretty crazy and a bit surreal here at the mansion, but the animals help us keep things in perspective and stay focused on the important aspects of life: unconditional love and support of one another.

"Things you might not know about Wednesday:

1. She was named after the little girl from *The Addam's Family*.
2. Her birthday is on April 12, making her an Aries.
3. She has a white stripe on her belly. She looks like an upside down skunk.
4. She has blond highlights underneath her black fur. I joke that it must be the Playboy water turning her blond.
5. She loves bell peppers!

"If I were in charge of the world, the first ruling that I would make on behalf of animals would be a law enforcing everyone to have their pets spayed or neutered.

"I am shocked and appalled to see and hear about the unbearable treatment that some commercial breeders impose on their animals. The conditions that these poor animals live in and the treatment they are forced to endure are horrendous and sickening. It will truly take the diligence and support of every animal lover to come together and take a stand to make these types of practices a thing of the past. **99**

BRENDAN BRAZIER
Ironman triathlete, author, with Teddy Sloan

Brendan Brazier is one of the few professional athletes in the world whose diet is 100 percent plant based. He's a professional Ironman triathlete, the bestselling author of *The Thrive Diet*, and the creator of an award-winning line of whole food nutritional products called VEGA. He is also the 2003 and 2006 Canadian 50km Ultra Marathon Champion and in 2007 was named by *VegNews* magazine as one of the "25 Most Fascinating Vegetarians."

66 At the age of fifteen, I decided that I wanted to become a professional Ironman triathlete. An Ironman race is made up of a 3.4-mile swim, a 112-mile bike ride, and a 26.2-mile run. Clearly, to be able to compete in an event such as this at a high-level, I'd have to train a huge amount. I quickly learned that proper nutrition complemented hard training, and that the combination would facilitate quicker fitness gains. But after experimenting with several different supposed performance-enhancing diets, I didn't notice greater fitness gains. Then I tried a properly balanced plant-based diet. It made a considerable difference. My recovery improved dramatically, so therefore I could train more. As a result I improved rapidly and started my professional career earlier than most other athletes.

"Though my motivation for not eating animals stemmed from health and performance consideration, what I've learned since has made my decision to eat a plant-based diet considerably more meaningful to me. Of course there are the dramatic environmental benefits that a vegan diet offers, so that pleases me. But there's also the matter of how animals raised for food are treated. As I grew increasingly interested in where my food came from, I knew for certain that I wanted no part in supporting the raising of animals for me to eat. This became especially significant since I had proven to myself that the absence of animal products in the diet was a tremendous health and performance benefit. Not only did my newly adopted plant-based diet enable me to perform at a higher level and help reduce my carbon footprint, it also put my mind at ease that I was no longer helping to sustain an industry that disregards the way animals are treated. 99

TAMAR GELLER
Author, *The Loved Dog*, with Clyde and Duke

As a former Israeli intelligence officer, Tamar Geller witnessed inhumane methods of dog training during her duty. Coupled with the abusive childhood that she herself suffered, she became sensitized to issues of cruelty, resulting in a career that is based on positive methods of training and mutual respect between dog and human. As Oprah's dog trainer, Tamar has reached millions with her message of love and reward training, as opposed to punishment and pain.

" Clyde and Duke are each a success story in rebuilding their broken souls and their broken trust in people. Clyde at about eight months was thrown out of a moving car, probably because he outgrew his cuteness as a puppy, but he still had some jumping and chewing issues. Duke is a survivor of a pit-bull fighting ring where he was used as bait. His back feet were broken so he would not be able to effectively defend himself. Somehow he was rescued and brought to the local shelter where I found him. I'm very lucky to have those two sweet beings in my life!

"Because of my and many of my clients' and friends' wonderful experiences with adopting shelter dogs, I want to help people share the joy of having rescued a dog. So many people are afraid to do so because they think, *I don't know what I'm getting*. But I have the solution. My foundation, The Loved World, is about cooperation between animals and people, where both sides help each other to love and live a better life. We sponsor a program where shelter dogs are trained by inmates in prison using *The Loved Dog* training method. Once they are certified as "a loved dog," they are available for adoption by the public. It's a breakthrough program as both prisoners and dogs experience the love and the power of communicating with no anger and violence. Those prisoners who are released are invited to become paid trainers at The Loved Dog training centers. "

It doesn't get much more embarrassing than this: We broke Todd's window at the shoot. Poor Elizabeth Sagarin, the photographer who took this shot, and one of Todd's staff, were moving furniture when suddenly I heard the hideous sound of breaking glass. In an effort to squeeze one of Todd's chairs past a tight spot, they pushed the arm into a huge window.

But here's how nice he is: When Elizabeth and I showed him that his enormous window had been shattered to smithereens, he smiled and said, "Don't worry. It's okay. Really." I whipped out my checkbook, but he refused to take a dime no matter how many times I asked.

So does it come as any surprise that on top of being one of the country's most talented designers, he's also a huge animal lover? Todd's adorable pup, Anne, is never far from his side, and I couldn't help but notice how exceptionally sweet she was. I know where she gets it from.

CARMINDY
Makeup artist, TLC's *What Not to Wear*

As the makeup host of *What Not to Wear,* Carmindy is the one who puts the important finishing touch on the woman of the hour. Stacey and Clinton would have already chucked her entire wardrobe, and Nick would have chopped off her locks. Now it's Carmindy's turn. Like a master painter, she transforms her canvas of an unremarkable face into a thing of beauty.

Yes, she's as lovely as she appears. And she taught me all sorts of great stuff—like, I was using eye shadow that was too pink and not warm enough for my skin tone. Hey, I need to escape from this work once in a while. I loved every girly minute of it!

Carmindy is the author of *The 5-Minute Face,* and her first makeup line, Sally Hansen Natural Beauty Inspired by Carmindy, is in drugstores nationwide and has *not* been tested on animals. Yay!

MARY MAX
Amimal welfare advocate

Mary Max, artist Peter Max's wife, was one of the first animal welfare advocates I met. It was Mary who asked me to watch two films that changed my life: *Life Behind Bars*, a thirteen-minute exposé of the nightmarish brutality of factory farming, narrated by Mary Tyler Moore, and *The Witness*, the true story of an unlikely animal advocate, a construction worker who had an epiphany about animals and the fur industry—as unlikely an advocate as Mary and I both were.

"When I met Peter, I had no regard for animals whatsoever, not even for cats or dogs. I just didn't think about them. When Peter announced one October morning that he was bringing home an orphaned two-week-old kitty, I vociferously protested! I didn't want our apartment filled with cat hair and litter. However, the second he came through our door and I saw that helpless being, motherly instincts flooded me. I bottle-fed her, bathed her in the cup of my hand, and slept with her nuzzled to my chest. Because she was so young, she needed me just like she would have needed her cat mom.

"Living with Miss October taught me that animals are more similar to us than different. They have two eyes, ears, a nose, a mouth, and, at turns, are playful, tired, hungry, cranky, and affectionate. Wow! Real desires, real interests, real emotions! So began my journey of thinking not only about Miss October but all animals. And what extraordinary things I learned. For instance, chickens are inquisitive animals who, in their natural surroundings, not on factory farms, form friendships and social hierarchies, recognize one another, love their young, and enjoy a full life. To learn that these and other sentient beings are imprisoned at factory farms, testing labs, fur farms, zoos, and so on, horrified me. I wanted to do something about it and so began my full-time volunteer life as an animal advocate.

"I joined Farm Sanctuary's No Veal Campaign, started an e-mail alert service, and screened such films as *The Witness* and *Peaceable Kingdom*. I lobby lawmakers regarding animal protection laws and am working to implement a resolution that allows plant-based meals in all New York State schools. I relish my role as a board member of The Humane Society of the United States, Humane USA, and the New York Coalition for Healthy School Lunches.

"In the midst of all of this, I have adopted seven rescued kitties and one dog, Maggie. Caring for and being a voice for animals has enriched my life in ways I never would have imagined. It has taken me on a spiritual and intellectual journey that, yes, is sometimes painful, but more often is deeply satisfying. I encourage anyone reading this book to take some time to get to know and speak up for our fellow earthly beings."

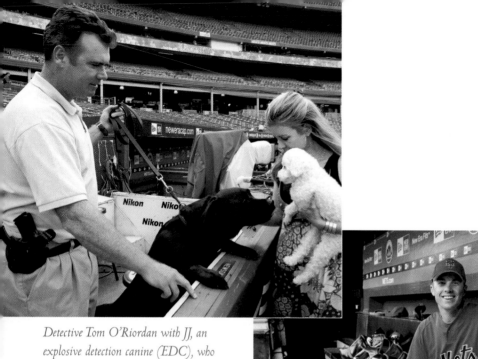

Detective Tom O'Riordan with JJ, an explosive detection canine (EDC), who protects fans and players at every game.

David Wright and Paul Lo Duca.

THE NEW YORK METS

On the scale of cool photo shoots this one was off the charts! All the players were so nice to Baby, and we even got to meet a hard-working police dog charged with the responsibility of making sure the ballpark is safe from explosives (sad, but true). It's quite a testament to their skill that dogs are entrusted with such an important job. To think how they are treated at puppy mills, when they do so much to protect us, is a disgrace.

Billy Wagner.

Ricky Henderson.

Paul Lo Duca giving Baby some love.

GARY FRETWELL
and Jill, owner of Twin Fires

On our way to the Berkshires I spied a sign from the road that said ANTIQUES. Not one to pass up the chance to shop, I cried, "Pull over!" At the end of a gravel road, a shop awaited us with the somewhat odd name of Twin Fires. A shopkeeper introduced himself and the store's resident dog, a sweet dachshund named Jill. When I asked how he came to acquire his pal (always hopeful it will be an adoption story), I was shocked to hear him say that not only was she a rescue, she had been an "orphan" of September 11. Someone had found her alone in an apartment, waiting in vain for her person to come home. Like other pets whose people died that day, she was put in a shelter, where Gary adopted her.

It was only weeks later, as I was looking at these photos, that I noticed the sign on the store, Twin Fires. I thought about Jill being an orphan as a result of the destruction of the Twin Towers, which had been twin fires in the end. I called Gary to ask him about that and he agreed that it was an eerie coincidence.

Bobby Jenks and Mark Buehrle (above), along with A. J. Pierzynski (right), are all big dog lovers. A. J. videotaped a public service announcement for us about puppy mills, including a plea for fans to rescue or adopt their next dog.

CHICAGO WHITE SOX

My home team! It was such a thrill to meet these great athletes. They were simply wonderful to Baby and eager to help spread the word about puppy mills.

AMY SEDARIS
Actress, author of *I Like You: Hospitality Under the Influence*, with Dusty

When I read Amy Sedaris's book, *I Like You: Hospitality Under the Influence*, I laughed so hard I snorted (and gasped at other times—see her illustration and lecture about personal hygiene and examining and cleaning yourself "down there"), and couldn't help but wonder what it must be like to go through life inside her head. Amy is a comic genius—either that or something we covered in a psychology course in grad school.

Baby tinkled on Amy's rug which, of course, mortified me. Between breaking Todd Oldham's window and Baby peeing on Amy Sedaris's rug, I feared that we were going to get quite the reputation. Amy and Todd are good friends, to boot, so I imagined a conversation that would end with both of them concluding that no good deed goes unpunished.

Amy, a fascinating comedian, writer, and actress, shares her unusual home with an animal of a different kind, but a rescue animal nonetheless!

Q: Your home is chock-full of animal tchotchkes—pictures, paintings, pillows, props—a veritable shrine to animals. And all the other stuff—fake meat hanging on the wall, fake lit cigarette resting in an ashtray—make your apartment look like the prop department of a movie studio, or a gag store. What's up with that?

A: *I surround myself with things I like. Everything has a story attached to it and it means something to me. It's personal and one of a kind. One thing I want to do before I die is to open my own prop and costume house. Cash only. I save everything.*

Q: Leave it to you to have an atypical pet! How and why did you decide to bring a rabbit into your life?

A: *I've always been drawn to rabbits. I saw my first rabbit, Tattletail, in a window and just decided today was the day I was going to bring her home. I'll always have a rabbit in my life. It's the perfect pet to bring your home alive. Lots of rabbits need rescuing and the best place to adopt a rabbit would be your local House Rabbit Society; these people are so dedicated to helping rabbits find homes. Nothing beats watching a prey animal kick back and relax in the comforts of your own home.*

Q: What has your relationship with Dusty taught you about yourself? About life?

A: *A lot of things really. I like the responsibility. We have so much in common—we both can see behind us, we both are rather jumpy, we love to eat, and we sleep with one eye open.*

Q: How are you and Dusty alike?

A: *We are both quick, curious, and considered prey.*

Q: Do you think of Dusty as a surrogate child?

A: *No, it's more like an abusive relationship. I like getting bossed around and used. She swindles me; it's a very codependent relationship. I am attracted to people similar to Dusty, and people like Dusty are attracted to me. It keeps you on your toes. We work.*

Q: What kind of animal would you want to come back as in your next life?

A: *Stuffed.*

At a rehearsal for the BET Spirit in Song concert, Baby got to take the stage with Patti.
Whenever I hear Patti sing, I can't help but be moved to tears.

PATTI LABELLE
Singer

Joel McHale makes me laugh. A lot. Joel and Lou, the show's resident hound (who belongs to coproducer Ed Boyd), were howling mad when they learned about puppy mills.

As for Baby, she wondered how many more of these photo shoots she'd have to endure. Lou's vocal talents were revealed when Ed was cleaning the house singing to Mariah Carey's "We Belong Together." "I was singing my heart out . . . thinking of a special someone . . . and Lou was there to make me laugh and take my mind off that person with his insane howling. I nearly peed my pants, I was laughing so hard," said Ed.

As soon as Mariel closed her eyes and began to relax into this pose, Baby left my side (which she rarely does) and spontaneously crawled into Mariel's lap, closing her own eyes. I had never seen her do that before. According to my yoga teacher, Jodi Blumstein, "It is said in India that if you practice yoga, you affect your family three generations forward and three generations back. That means that yoga and meditation have profound and long-reaching effects. I often imagine how peaceful our world would be if everyone meditated, and how much less cruelty and abuse there would be toward all creatures."

"The Quiet Dogs"
by Mariel Hemingway

I AWAKEN AT around 5:45 a.m. to feel the softness of early morning and listen to the lack of human sounds that will soon fill the world. This important quiet start of the day defines how I approach the rest of it. The morning is cool, and even in Los Angeles I need a sweater or scarf in the early hours. I go outside, feel the chill, and smell the blossoms of my Meyer lemon tree. I look for the "perfect" place to sit.

An old oak tree, which has clearly seen more change in this neighborhood than anyone playing under her branches in the last seven years, looks more inviting than ever. I set a cushion down, just so, next to her massive trunk and I sit myself heavy into the ground. I root the base of my spine to the roots of my golden oak.

As soon as I have settled in, I am joined by Bindu, my fierce and muscle-bound Yorkie. No small-dog complex here, he thinks he has the rights to the center of my lap, along with the right to orchestrate the defense of our home. He finds his place in the center of my folded legs, and Pimple, yes, that's right, Pimple, backs up into my lap in front of me. A delicate teacup Yorkie, Pimple literally looks behind him and backs his feet into Bindu's face and nudges into his "rightful" place next to the warmth of my belly. Bindu doesn't mind (he just curls around his partner), because frankly, Pimple may be more wife than buddy to Bindu, as they are constantly together, share their food, and sleep in the same snuggle zone, whether protecting each other from a cold gust of wind or just relaxing after a grueling hike with Mom (yeah, that's me). Also, they bitch at one another in a married way. You know, as Bindu would say, "I can call her a bitch but you, my friend (that would be any other dog they encounter), will get a hunk of your ear missing if you cross her."

Two small dogs settled and I begin to tune into the cacophony of morning sounds. Birds call out to each other the dangers and interests of the day. I smile in recognition of their voices, while the babes in my lap are instantly too deep into bliss to be disturbed. Then comes Bondi, she is my rescued Belgian sheepdog, and she lands close to me but with great consideration of my space. She knows she is there to defend and that I feel her close by. I open my eyes and give her a grateful glance for her quiet intensity. She is all elegance and poise. She remains awake and sniffing the air in search of anything predatory. The whities, my two Maltese, have been checking out the yard during this time, mostly searching for food, which they both seem to think will have fallen from the sky the night before. When their search fails, Wicklow makes his way toward me, begins to wiggle in and promptly begins a growling standoff. Bindu doesn't even move his head but lets his adversary know he is there, guarding his wife, and you, my friend, are out of luck. Wicky does a little dance for me and snaps at Bindu then takes off at a sprint to his blanket next to the door. Bindu knows his best attention comes when his momma (my seventeen-year-old daughter) wakes up, and hours of grooming and petting begin—he can wait.

That leaves Pep. An energetic Maltese with a big heart. She is always in search of love but doesn't outwardly ask for it. Instead she makes her way to my arm, gives it a lick and a nibble, telling me she is there but in no way wants to interrupt me. I stop for a second and give her an approving look and a scratch behind her ears; relieved, she sits down near but not touching me. She knows that if she is quickly quiet, breakfast will come faster, so profound is her meditation.

In silent observation of all that is close to me, their sounds drift from my awareness. I feel gratitude that I begin my every day with such humble servants of Mother Nature. In their furry spots I feel that they are more connected to solitude, acceptance, and compassion than I will ever be. Unconditional in their absolute existence, not just in love, they are my teachers.

VICTORIA STILWELL

Host of Animal Planet's *It's Me or the Dog*, author of *It's Me or the Dog: How to Have the Perfect Pet*, with rescue dog Bosco

Whenever I see someone walking a dog with a chain or prong collar, it looks like a medieval torture device. If people tried them on their own necks, and gave them a good yank, they would realize how painful and cruel these collars are. I also cringe when I see the harness type of lead around a dog's muzzle, because too often the dog can't open his mouth enough to pant, which he needs to do to regulate his body temperature.

When I asked Victoria Stilwell, the host of Animal Planet's *It's Me or the Dog*, and an advocate for the Wisconsin Puppy Mill Project, she agreed that prong and choke collars should be *banned*. As for the harness type that fits over the muzzle, she agreed that if not fitted properly, allowing the dog to open his jaws enough, it can be less than humane, but if fitted right, it can be okay as a temporary training tool, *but only for training* (if it makes an indentation on the muzzle, it's too tight). For any of you still using these collars, please read on:

"Training with Kindness, Not Cruelty"
by Victoria Stilwell

THERE IS NO place in training for the choke or prong/pinch collar. These metal collars are designed to inflict considerable pain and discomfort if the dog pulls. Those who advocate their use say that it takes one "pop" on the choke chain and then the dog walks well, because if he pulls again, he fears that the same painful sensation will occur. This might be true in some cases, but unfortunately what the dog has just been taught is that walking causes pain—and the pain is linked to the owner!

There are also some dogs that will endure the pain and keep pulling, however much the choke collar is cutting into the dog's neck, making it difficult for him to breathe. You just have to look at a dog's bloodshot eyes to see that the choke collar is slowly strangling him. Fast forward a couple of months or even years, and the dog may find itself at the veterinarian with a severely damaged trachea or worse: non-cardiogenic pulmonary edema (water on the lungs) due to temporary upper airway obstruction. This has become an increasingly common condition for dogs that are walked with choke chains, and in many cases the damage is immediate.

A head collar is a device that can help to stop a dog from pulling. A strap is fitted around the dog's muzzle and another strap rests just behind the ears. Once on, the dog finds it harder to pull because as soon as any pressure is put on the head collar, the dog's head automatically comes round. These head collars are a much safer option, as they distribute weight evenly around the head and muzzle area, taking pressure off a dog's delicate throat.

However, head collars also come with drawbacks. If a dog wearing a head collar suddenly lunges, the neck can snap around and the collar can cause physical damage. Many dogs don't like having a strap around the muzzle, as it is a strange sensation and might make the dog more anxious and therefore fear walking. Owners also tend to fit the head collar incorrectly, pulling the muzzle strap too tight or in many cases fitting the head collar so loosely that the dog can easily get out of it. If fitted correctly, the dog should be able to open his mouth to take treats, pant, vomit, or drink water. Care should also be taken when first introducing the head collar to a dog, and time should be spent getting the dog used to the feeling of something on his face. If the head collar is paired with a nice tasty treat while being fitted, the dog can begin to look forward to wearing it.

Harnesses that are specially designed to stop pulling also are available. Unlike normal harnesses, these harnesses make it more difficult for the dog to pull because as he does, he feels like his front legs are being hoisted off the ground. Two straps that tighten under the front legs cause this sensation. This also has drawbacks. Chafing can occur under the "armpits," and muscle damage has been reported when these harnesses have been used for long periods of time.

So what do you use to stop a dog from pulling? It's called training, and there is no substitute for taking the time to train your dog to walk well on a leash using positive, reward-based methods rather than relying on a quick fix. Head collars and harnesses that help to stop pulling are okay to use in the short term if fitted and used correctly, but should be only an aid to training and should never be considered a long-term solution. Walking should be enjoyable for dog and owner, and with time and patience, any dog can be taught to walk well on the lead with just a regular collar.

Training is about giving a dog the ability to live successfully in a human world. This is not done by "dominating" a dog and making him submit to you, numbing any negative responses with harsh methods that don't treat the underlying cause of the behavior. It's about using positive reinforcement (rewarding behavior that you want the dog to repeat) to give a dog the confidence he needs to live successfully in our domestic environment, and fostering a mutually respectful and beneficial relationship that strengthens the bond between dog and owner. I remain deeply committed to education as a means to achieve this, including teaching children how to effectively communicate with and understand dogs, empowering kids with the knowledge that helps them to be safe, responsible, and compassionate, not just toward dogs but to all animals.

CHYNNA PHILLIPS and BILLY BALDWIN
Recording artist and actor

Chynna and Billy are big animal lovers who dote on Thurman, a beloved member of their family. An exceptionally gracious host to Baby, Thurman was clearly nonchalant about the prospect of becoming a celebrity like his mom and dad.

Before we began, Jack (center) asked if he could be the one to hold Baby for the shot.

THE ANAHEIM DUCKS
and the ST. LOUIS CARDINALS

Chris Pronger of the Anaheim Ducks and son Jack, who, at age five, already shows signs of his dad's talent on the ice.

During the shoot, Chris's wife, Lauren, was nice enough to call their neighbors, the Edmonds, and asked them to come over. They turned out to be Jim Edmonds of the St. Louis Cardinals and his wife, Alison. Jim agreed to pose with Baby. He had left his bat at the Prongers' house awhile back, so it was there, ready for the shot.

Baby was a special guest at a benefit for Farm Sanctuary, where Moby performed.

MOBY
Recording artist

LORETTA SWIT
Actress, animal advocate

❝ People have asked me over the years about when or if I experienced a 'moment' of deciding to become an actress or an activist in the humane community. I wish I had some dramatic and meaningful story to tell, but truthfully, I do not. What I recall is never having any doubts about the commitment and passion I have for the arts and for the love, care, and preservation of life on this planet. Just recently I read that 'passion is able to turn the ordinary into the extraordinary.' I am roused to speak for those who cannot speak for themselves, and an inspired even more by the courage of Baby, who not only cannot speak, but *also* has no voice. The passion I share with you for the plight of animals globally will not diminish until we recognize that we are caretakers here . . . and it is for us to take care of every sentient being on this planet. ❞

Only in New York— the Mt. Everest of p-mail!

In prison we weren't allowed to get p-mail, so when I was finally released, it was a dream come true to discover that I had mail waiting for me everywhere. Every few steps there'd be another one to read and answer. My replies just flowed, and even at the end of my walks, when I thought I couldn't possibly answer another, somehow I'd manage to eke out one more, even if only to say "hi" or "later." Everyone's cool with that. We understand how demanding one another's schedules are—pee, poop, eat, sleep, play, and start all over again. Life on the outside is sweet.

We're lucky—you two-leggers need a machine to answer your p-mail. And when was the last time that you sat down to answer your first p-mail of the day and said, "Ahhhhhhhhhh!"?

"Hey, look, Ma—that's me!"

Never doubt that a small group of
thoughtful, committed citizens can
change the world. Indeed, it is the
only thing that ever has.

—MARGARET MEAD

Chapter 7

You, Wonderful You

It's amazing how much my perspective has changed since the time when I considered a rescue dog as second best. Now that I've known the joys of living with an adopted dog, I wouldn't and couldn't have anything else. Since that time, I've made an important discovery: The bonding you have with an animal that you save is beyond anything you could imagine. The way a rescue dog looks at you is different from a dog that you buy as a puppy. Their history is precisely what makes them so special. Give me a dog who is interesting, who has character and substance! Even more, they are extraordinarily loving, adoring, and eager to please, so grateful to be given a second chance that they pull out all the stops in wooing you. A dog who you have adopted from a shelter, or taken in from the streets, or saved from an abusive situation, looks into your eyes with such intense love, gratitude, and wonderment, it's as if she thinks you're some kind of walking miracle. When you're on the receiving end of that look, you know that only rescue dogs are in your future. The mutual understanding of each other's inherent value is all too clear. The rescued needs the rescuer; but the rescuer equally needs the rescued. I've come to understand that our highest purpose is to ease the suffering of others, including the animals in our midst who are mistreated.

They are, after all, completely at our mercy, unable to report when they are being abused or neglected. Unable to say, "Please help me. Please give me a forever home. I promise it will be the best decision you ever made." How can we turn away?

I was pretty lazy in gym class. When we had to run around the track, I'd stop running when the teacher wasn't looking, thinking *This is such a schlep! Why do we have to do this?*

But now I feel like an Olympic athlete—a runner in a relay race who has been passed the baton by one of the many animal-welfare advocates who came before me, extending the torch to me in the hopes that I might grab it, run like hell with it, and pass it on to another. I have tried to do exactly that. Sometimes I offer it to someone and they drop it to the ground; other times they grab it and take off running full speed. My hope is that this book will take on the appearance of a baton for you, that it will inspire you to do something, even a seemingly small act like adopting or rescuing a dog instead of buying one from a breeder. That one act of compassion would be a huge step toward putting puppy mills and inhumane backyard breeders out of business. Not to mention that each year in this country roughly four million dogs are killed because there are not enough homes for them. That means that every time you buy a dog instead of adopting one, you are signing the death sentence of a dog in a shelter. And if you care about economics, you should know that it costs us taxpayers $2 billion a year to round up, shelter, euthanize, and dispose of homeless animals. So, every time you buy a dog from a breeder, as opposed to adopting one, you are contributing to an obscene waste of valu-

able resources that could be otherwise used to help children, the poor, or any number of worthy social service programs.

Being part of the solution instead of part of the problem feels fantastic. Rescued dogs know they have been saved, and they'll reward you a million times over in ways you never imagined. The joy I get from Baby's gratitude is something I wish all of you might have the chance to experience, too.

You're a great person. That's why you bought a book about a three-legged dog, a book in which all of my profits from the sale of this book go to the HSUS. And that's why you adopted a homeless dog yourself. You didn't? Well, I still like you because I think there's hope for you yet. In fact, I'll bet that after you read my list of reasons why you should adopt a dog, you'll be ready to join this very privileged club.

Top ~~Ten~~ Eleven Reasons Why Adopting a Dog Is so Much Better Than Buying One from a Breeder

1. It's good karma. If you adopt a dog in this life, you won't come back as a breeding dog at a puppy mill in your next life.
2. Shelter dogs' toes smell like popcorn. You don't believe me? Go ahead and adopt a dog and smell their toes on the way home. If I'm lying, a year's worth of popcorn on me.
3. It builds character—related to the #1 reason but relevant for this life, not a future one!
4. Martina Navratilova will be your friend—well, the odds are greatly increased (see pages 122–123).
5. I will be your friend.
6. Shelter dogs are usually past the puppy stage, meaning you won't come home to find that your favorite and very expensive shoes have been shredded to bits by razor-sharp puppy teeth.

7. You'll know with 100 percent certainty that you won't be supporting a cruel puppy mill or inhumane backyard breeder.

8. Your IQ will go up several points. It's true. After I adopted Baby, I felt so much smarter than the people I knew who were still buying dogs from breeders.

9. You will be worshipped and revered for the first time in your life.

10. There's a pup out there who desperately needs you, and if you buy a dog from a breeder you are signing a death warrant for one who needs a home.

And the last, and most important, reason to adopt a shelter dog . . .

11. You'll lose weight. Well, you might. Nothing else has worked, so why not give it a try.

The first place to look for your own special Baby is at the local shelter or pound. There are wonderful, lovable pups there, just waiting for their forever home. Many are ideal in temperament and physical health, but may have been the victims of irresponsible owners or unfortunate circumstances. Take time to see if one pulls at your heartstrings.

Another great source, and where I found Baby, is at Petfinder.com, or 1-800-Save-a-Pet.com. Wait until you see the thousands of available pups—one more lovable and adorable than the next. Hold on a second. While I have you here, I want to take a quick look at Petfinder.com to see if there's anyone as cute as her for you. . . .

I'm back. All I can say is: Oh boy, are you gonna have a tough time choosing. The first little darling I saw when I entered a search for Yorkies in New York was a girl named Angel, with the biggest, most expressive eyes I've ever seen. She's four and as sweet as sugar. Next I did a search in St. Louis and came across a stunner named Buddy, who is also four and loves children and other dogs. He was a cross between a cocker spaniel and a poodle and looked like a movie star. Finally, I did a search for Chihuahuas in Miami and came across a little boy—Are you sitting down?—named *Popcorn!* I can't even imagine how delicious *his* toes smell—like the front of the concession line at a movie theater. He's five and loves to be held and cuddled.

As you can see, Petfinder.com or 1-800-Save-a-Pet.com is a great way to find your baby, but you can also do an online search for rescue groups that deal with specific breeds. Do a search for "Chihuahua rescue" or "Cocker spaniel rescue" and you'll find people who specialize in whatever breed you like. But be open. Don't assume you know exactly the breed you want. Mixed breed dogs are often less prone to genetic disorders and, like mixed breed humans, are often the most gorgeous. You may come home with an unexpected treasure who will be the angel of your life. I always find that when I put aside my preconceived ideas and am open, I get rewarded beyond my expectations.

Most important, please don't ever buy from a pet store or an Internet puppy site or a breeder that you have not personally visited. NEVER. If you do, odds are you will be supporting animal cruelty. No matter how cute that puppy is, think of his parents, who may be suffering horrrific abuse.

Unless you visit a breeder's operation in person, you can assume the worst. As is often the case with pet store owners, many puppy mill breeders are less than forthcoming about the living conditions and treatment of their breeding dogs. Countless consumers have reported being told, "I'm not a puppy mill breeder," only to find out the grim reality when they investigated further or visited the site in person. If you are told that the breeding dogs are part of the family and are free to run and play outdoors, you must go there to see for yourself. Don't let a breeder e-mail you photos. Many people report receiving photos of dogs frolicking in yards or bucolic settings only to discover the sad truth when they insisted on visiting in person—rows of cages or kennels where breeding dogs spend all or most of their time locked up like prisoners.

I'll say it again: The only way to know for sure whether a breeder is humane is to see the facility for yourself. If they have more than a few breeding dogs, that's a *red flag!* Owning more than several breeding dogs likely means they are in it for money, and if that's the case, they are likely to be churning out puppies as fast and as often as they can, thereby compromising the treatment of their breeding dogs.

If a breeder agrees to ship you a puppy in the cargo section of a plane, that's a *red flag!* Any breeder who would ship a puppy in the hold of an airplane doesn't give a hoot about the animal's welfare. The terror a puppy experiences during a trip in the underbelly of a plane is beyond extreme, and the potential dangers are great. They can be subjected to extreme temperatures and noise levels, and sometimes are dead upon arrival.

If a breeder discourages you from coming to visit, that's a *red flag!* Any breeder who isn't willing or able to be completely transparent in their operations and their treatment of their dogs is hiding something—namely, mistreatment of the breeding dogs.

If a breeder doesn't screen and interview you very carefully and/or do a home check, that's a *red flag!* Humane breeders who love their dogs are very cautious about prospective buyers. If they don't give you the third degree, that means they couldn't care less about the fate of the puppies they're selling. Think about it: Would a responsible, caring, and humane breeder just hand over their puppies to a pet store or sell them on the Internet to strangers they will never meet? Not on your life, they wouldn't.

If you are hell-bent on buying from a breeder despite my pleas to do otherwise, then you *must* visit the place in person and do a thorough investigation of how the breeding dogs are treated. You *cannot* take their word for it over the phone or by e-mail. Go see for yourself if the breeding dogs are part of the family, or if they are locked in cages like condemned criminals. But I'm assuming that if you're still reading this, you're seriously considering adoption, and if so, you are the coolest. Hooray for you! Hooray for the pup who you are about to fall in love with! As you're looking at the listings on Petfinder.com or 1-800-Save-a-Pet.com, don't overlook the older dogs, who are my favorites. There are so many pros to adopting an older dog. They have more to give than a puppy—more depth, more soul, more heart.

Personally, I don't want to deal with the nonstop hyperactivity and craziness of a puppy. I like my peace and quiet when I'm home and alternately have a full and active life. A puppy is so demanding and so hyper—you never have a moment's peace except when they're sleeping. And even then you're holding your breath, waiting for them to suddenly spring into action all over again. Give me an adult dog who is calmer and able to chill with me.

Then there's the destructive side of a puppy. They need and want to chew everything, including your new purse and your gorgeous throw pillows. Those razor-sharp puppy teeth will rip through things faster than a Ginzu knife.

No thanks. Been there.

I love that Baby was nearly ten when I adopted her (my wonderful cat Kitty Pie was fourteen). Senior pets are the least likely to find a forever home. So they are the ones I'm most drawn to. Those are the ones who need me. Imagine them being in their golden years with nowhere to go, but still with so much to give. I say, put your feet up here, girl. You deserve to have a forever home just as much as the one- and two-year-olds. Come rest your tired head on my lap. You're home now.

Taking Action!

The puppy-mill owners are many and their lobbyists are powerful, but you and I can have the last word. We can take back the power from those who abuse it. You are very powerful. More than you know.

Senators, congressmen, city council members, and state attorney generals have all told me the same thing: Calls and e-mails to their office do, indeed, make a big impact. We must never doubt that one call or e-mail has the power to change the world for the better. I remember when I placed a call to my congressman about a pending horse-slaughter bill. I told the staffer who answered the phone that I was calling to urge the congressman to vote in favor of a ban on horse slaughter. I asked the young man if he had received similar calls that day.

"You have no idea!" he exclaimed. "There sure are a lot of horse lovers out there!" I smiled as I hung up, grateful to all those callers who, like me, decided to take thirty seconds to pick up the phone and make their opinion known. If there had been any question in that congressman's mind before, he was now crystal clear about how he should vote. We cannot say to ourselves, *There will be plenty of others making calls and writing e-mails— my one measly call won't make a difference.* Not true. We simply can't pass the buck. The animals are depending on each and every one of us to do something to help them. *Now.*

We must remember that the people who love and care about animals far outnumber the bad guys who hurt them. Our collective voices can drown out theirs every time, if we choose to speak up. And that includes the billion-dollar corporations who abuse animals. Their wealth and influence, though vast, will not match the swell of negative public opinion that will occur when their inhumane practices come to light.

You don't have to become a full-time activist to make an impact. Even the quickest and simplest of acts—a quick call or an e-mail to your senators, congressman, and state attorney general—can make all the difference. Don't be embarrassed if you don't know who your elected representatives are. There was a time when I didn't either. It's easy to find out. To contact your two U.S. senators, go to www.Senate.gov. To contact your congressman in the U.S. House of Representatives, go to www .House.gov.

The Humane Society of the United States is doing great things for animals in so many areas, and they need your help. Please visit their site at www.HumaneSociety.org and get involved! They are waiting to welcome you into the HSUS family.

I Hate Good-byes . . . So Let's Say "Hello"

It's been quite a ride, but now comes the most important part of this journey. Shutting down those houses of horror known as puppy mills. Please call and write your two senators, your congressman, and state attorney general. Tell them you want them to shut down puppy mills. Get ten friends to do the same and ask if each of them can get ten friends. You will see. We can do this. We must. Thousands of innocent prisoners, locked away and left to suffer a lifetime of abuse, are depending on us.

Thank you, friend, for caring so much and for having a great, big, beautiful heart. Because of you, we will see a better day for all creatures—small and big—since our treatment of one informs the other.

Baby and I would *love* to hear from you. To contact us, sign up for free newsletters, and get the scoop about other cool stuff, like Baby's fantastic, toe-tappin' animal album and plush toy in her likeness, please visit us at www.RareBreedofLove.com.

With love, gratitude, and hope,
Jana and Baby 🐾

"The End"

Photo Credits

p. 93 by Nancy Baily

p. 177 by Diane Beifeld

pp. 152, 179, 181 © Jessica Brooks (www.jessicabrooksphoto.com)

pp. 136, 178 by Brie Childers

pp. 182, 186, 187 by Steve Cohn

pp. 153, 164 by Cynthia Daniel (www.cynthiadanielphotographer.com)

p. 154 courtesy of Farm Sanctuary

p. 121 by Larry Ford (www.fordphotography.com)

p. 151 by Josh Freiwald

pp. 16, 80 by Steve Grubman

pp. xix, xx, 11, 14, 15, 25, 26, 27, 34, 35, 36, 37, 38, 39, 40, 41, 46, 48, 75, 79, 83, 84, 91, 97, 104, 107, 112, 113, 114, 118, 124, 128, 147, 158, 173 (bottom), 189, 190, 192, 202 by Bryan Harrell

p. 143 © 2005 by Gregory Heisler

pp. 22, 30, 88, 102, 116, 122, 137, 144, 146, 148, 167, 170, 171, 172, 174, 188, back jacket (Heather Mills and Billy Wagner) by Gerri Hernández

pp. 3, 51 courtesy of the Humane Society of the United States

pp. 10, 106, 130 by Jana Kohl

p. 129 © 2006 by Blake Little

p. 194, "Mutts" © Patrick McDonnell—Distributed by King Features Syndicate

pp. 138, 139 by Gitte Meldgaard

pp. 126, 127, back jacket (Lindsay Lohan) by Metin Oner

p. 47, cartoon from "Bizarro" by Dan Piraro. Used with permission.

p. 53 courtesy of Prisonersofgreed.org

pp. 131, 140, 156, 162, 166, 168 by Elizabeth Sagarin (www.zgorinphoto.com)

pp. 32, 67, 71, 72 (top), 73, 76, 77, 82, 108, 110, 119, 159, 185, back jacket (Barack Obama and Judge Judy) by Robert Sebree

p. 173 (top) by Jamie Slade

p. 42 by Tori Soper

p. 51 by Amanda Sorvino

pp. xviii, 9 by Pete Stenberg

pp. 59, 63, 68, 69, 70, 72 (bottom), 74, back jacket (Elizabeth Dole) by George Tolbert